THE SANCTITY OF RHYME:
The Metaphysics of Crying 4 Kafka
in Prose and Verse

THE SANCTITY OF RHYME:
The Metaphysics of Crying 4 Kafka
in Prose and Verse

Erika Blair

Asylum 4 Renegades Press
Joshua Tree, California

ASYLUM 4 RENEGADES PRESS
Joshua Tree, California
asylum4renegadespress.com

A4R seeks daring projects of interest to academic and
educated readers. A4R admires risk-taking authors who write
with intelligence and grace while remaining self-effacing
and wryly humorous.

Cover Art and Book Design
Tania Love Abramson
50yrslater.com

First Edition

DEDICATION

To My Wife Amantine

Crying 4 Kafka is a band. This is a band narrative
that eschews narration.

Preamble

Erika Blair
The Americana Desolation Music Academy
Joshua Tree, California

You're right. Right you are. The silence was deafening. Mocking, notorious, primeval. Desolate as only truth can be. Void of self-consciousness, while missions and motives unravel, like characters in fiction, amazed by the obstinacy of their addictions and predilections. Our consolation, if indeed it is a consolation, is to tell ourselves that we want something more than soporific platitudes and melodies born of complacency, that indefinable something well beyond the transience of pleasant tonal vibrations that cultivate the company of homesick somnambulists in a fog of gilded reverie.

A punk rock band perhaps, casting stories, largely autobiographical, delivered like grimacing canals, or evaporating dreams, emerging from the circles of hell, strangely aching, with sonic force and irony, whereby spirits, the penumbra of epiphanies, descend upon thinking brains set adrift, while iconoclasts are feted and crowned.

Stravinsky said, said he did, before tackling *Sacre du Printemps* that he wanted to refresh himself, to let himself go, thoughtless I assume, by composing something else, an orchestral maneuver as a lark in which the piano would dominate. Stravinsky had in mind, in his mind he had, an image, a metaphor, of a puppet coming to life, driving an orchestra crazy, with diabolical arpeggios. The orchestra, not to be outdone, or outmaneuvered, then retaliates with trumpet blasts. It's terrific noise Stravinsky said.

Perhaps you admire the rightness of the tone. The fantastic image, a puppet gone awry morphed into sound. The appropriateness of the emotion, the unrestrained indignation, the instinctive scorn. Was it instinctive? Must Kafka cry differently?

Piteous technologies that aspire and corrupt, and the social mediums that dazzle in their wake, reduce the coterie of ancestors to noble savages, drudges with happy faces. The Decline of the Roman Composition in an age of electronic purity is now celebrated with corrosive algorithms and serious bifocals to manipulate fastballs and sliders that unfold with check-lists compiled by seditious publishing conglomerates, anagrams and Auntie Sam, estranged and deranged continuously for posterity.

I am told, or so I am lead to believe, that Adele habituates songs through Tupperware parties, imposters sitting in separate rooms concocting jingles cut-up style, scissors purchased from Burroughs, sanitized or bleached, I can't remember which, until KGB agents emerge waving epiladys while memorizing *How to Pick Up Girls*. Hardly viable in the face of mad noise.

Rolling dice and *I Ching, Chinging* along isn't any better, though Johnny Von thinks otherwise, unstinting and masquerading as a Noblesse *Oblomov* for 4 minutes and 33 seconds while speed reading the *Leaves of Grass*, or was it Gunter Grass, tin drums and silent pasts. Landscapes with advanced degrees and cages looking for birds with no rhyme or reason for common denominators or fabricated muses conceived in tea-leaves of public disgraces humming *Surface Water on the Face of the Moon* and *Migration Bound Neurotransmitters*.

Accessible, danceable, canned and blind, fixed narratives, elixirs and woo-woo hooks transmuting musical syntax into elevators on the way down. Passing Turing machines and Kabbalists promising afternoon delights for high crimers and misdemeanors as a restless polygram with multiple tongues stumbled upon a shepherd, a steward of sorts, with crested geese and castles in the sand, stammering and jammering with channels, dials and crocodiles, grieving a legendary fall from grace and a misplaced ukulele in the key of S.

Vices and spices close at hand, Milton was pressed into liberation from an aggregate of reason, and then enslaved and depraved by the sanctity of rhyme. Lost and found, come hither, come yonder, *Comus*, come on, don't step on my blue suede shoes. Visions of Plato playin' tricks when I'm tryin' to be quiet, pretending to hasten towards a forbidden home, tipping hats to dead souls, forgetting abstinence and ne're-do-wells, while riding on the D train to Wrightsville.

TWO THINGS INTERTWINED
DESTINY IS COLOR-BLIND
SAME THINGS GUARANTEED
FAIRY-KINGS ON BENDED KNEES

WOULDA BET A SURE THING
SHINING LIKE A DIAMOND RING
THIS ONE COULD NEVER FAIL
JUST LIKE THE FAIRY TALE

THESE STORIES SOMETIMES END
TRAGEDY AROUND THE BEND
SHINING HIGH EVER BRIGHT
NEVER MAKES IT THRU THE NIGHT

SOMETIMES
YOU ROLL THE DICE

SOMETIMES
YOU ROLL THE DICE

SOMETIMES
YOU ROLL THE DICE

AND IT AIN'T ALWAYS
PARADISE

crying 4 kafka

ain't always paradise

Play the game not to lose; worried speeches disapproved; repertories on the run; gambits for Mr. Donne; feathers gathered for a feast; blind maps for a priest; beauty's beauty of the world; hurling through undisturbed.

Dadaism holds a gun; incomprehensible from above; marriage temples trembling now; lovers' lovers' lovers' love. Clarinets waving swords; bulletproof avant-garde; backwards, forward, fair enough; intuitions matters not.

Dancing for a certain crowd; smiling crooked with a bow; plastic Jesus on a hat; pidgin Proust acrobat; never troubles prophesy; on the charts of history; more and more for me to see; telescopic sophistry.

I will not tell a lie
I will not tell a lie
I will not cry
I will not cry
Oh my oh my
Oh my oh my

James Dean, Barney too; Haley Street coming thru. Jim Dine on the line; Mister Judd doin' fine. Red Room Eric said; turn a corner harlot's bed. Mirror, mirror on the wall; clavichord in the stall.

14

Virgil Thompson on the plains, river, river not to blame, *Symphony of the Air*, Leonardo doesn't care. Music, music then said; then, then yet again; revolution subtle first; mind, mind unrehearsed.

Homer tried, tried his hand; imagination in a band; readers hear then they see; welcome goddess, welcome she. Achilles, Achilles wants his prize. Agamemnon does despise. Hector too wants revenge. Achilles rises once again.

At his heal arrows fly; fifty men electrify; wooden horse lost its way; Arrakis on boxing-day. Me, me, said the muse; piercing camels through a storm; Cornell boxes from afar; sacking Troy in its prime.

Many saw forgotten moon; heard eclipse thinkin' too; pains, pains in the sea; struggle, struggle I agree. Homecoming waited for; 50 years never more; hard to hard twenty-five; reckless night did survive.

Fools, fools oxen bled; bullfighting from a sled; Sun God's rode away; Z's daughter here to play. Homecoming yet again; tried once to attend; never wanted anymore; fable, fable I abhor.

NO ONE EVER KNOWS THE PRICE THE SOLDIER PAYS UNTIL THE GIFT THE SOLDIER MAKES ENDS IN SHALLOW GRAVES

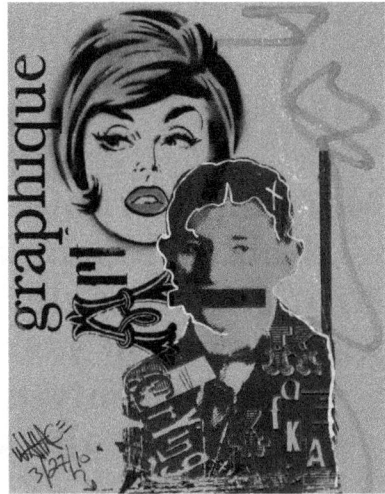

Never wanted, could not be; Huckleberry in ivory; knowledge down, down below; chasing tigers on a string. Chanting choirs turn away; luminaries get it more; 15 times Andy said; go to war letterhead; contemplating strangers when; turning worlds in a fix; around the dark, around the light; vernal flowers in a crowd.

Mortal existence holding hands; Kon Vics launch a band; clamor, clamor, hear it now; grey, grey run away; nothing shaded, nothing gained; acumen for a click; ruminations hide and seek; due, due yes they do.

Primal acts imagined not; signers, signers run away; revolution then declared; addicts snore in their prayers. Come, come another day; friends, friends gather here; like, like, like some more; fill the void with a fugue. Fill the void with a fugue. Fill the void with a fugue. Fill the void with a fugue.

✳✳✳✳✳✳✳✳✳✳✳✳✳✳✳

Pious I: A blessing and a curse, words retreat and intersperse.

Pious II: Autodidact looming from a well; waving charms found near hell; conducting episodes hopeless now; vexations, vexations trouble more; except of course Satie said; praying at the Chapel Read.

Fugazi: Escaping crimes from within. Is that what this is all about? Stretching words to fit music, or is it the other way around? Clairvoyance, parable, allegory? Inconceivable incantations and thesis upon thesis? What if we never know? What if it has a life of its own?

Yeats: High horses serve no one. You may drive away belittlements, scrupulous and capacious as they might be, but please keep in mind, they must be tempered for exorcism.

YOU'RE OUT OF YOUR FUCKIN' MIND
YOU'RE OUT OF YOUR FUCKIN' MIND

Fugazi: Why should we submit to the denigration of imagination? I don't care, really, I don't care. So what if it conflicts with or supersedes modernism or deviates from a preordained gospel or a Platonic ideal? Is there an imperative that we must follow? Are we all wounded ghosts with canned laughter? There's no everlasting formula.

Yeats: I'm not saying there is a key or code or single-minded interpretive precept. Those things are mercifully missing. All I ask for – ask for as I do – are searing introspections coupled with self-defining clues. Visceral perceptions are nice too.

I'LL HAVE YOUR ASS SUCKIN' SAND
I'LL HAVE YOUR ASS SUCKIN' SAND

Butthole Surfers: We are made of song, of song we are made. Only in this way can we, can we ever, persevere.

Emerson: Explication is an intrusion, a false caprice. This is my authorial warning.

Butthole Surfers: It's a limitless web of intrusion, but let's not mince words either. Songs are excavated, not spontaneous emissions. They may be robustly predetermined, but they transcend and are cultivated to do so.

Emerson: What about the question of language? The trapped beasts; the impossibility of knowing.

GET RID OF THAT FUCKIN' WHOREHOUSE ON WHEELS

GET RID OF THAT FUCKIN' WHOREHOUSE ON WHEELS

WHAT'S THE STORY I'M TRYING TO TELL
ROUND AND ROUND LIKE A CAROUSEL
FACE THE FEAR WITHOUT REGRET
BEYOND THE SHADOW OF
MY SILHOUETTE

EASY AT FIRST I DECLARED
PISTOL ROSE TO THE AUCTIONEER
MATTER SAID, PURPOSE FOUL
RAPID VOICE DISEMBOWELED

DEMONS COME, DEMONS GO
STEP ASIDE, LET THEM FLOW
DEMONS COME, DEMONS GO
STEP ASIDE, LET THEM FLOW

Patti Smith: That pace, that tone, the turns of phrase, transmuting form and syntax, burdened and Bergen as it were, empty maxims and weak metaphors.

Srinivasa Ramanujan: There are no Peers, not even a Mountain King will suffice, or Goethe for that matter. They must resolve the anti-hero's composition.

Patti Smith: What if the problem is the unassailable root of his tongue? A family legacy casually observed, like Ibsen, or was it Chekov?

Srinivasa Ramanujan: I share the conundrum. It's infinite. But who am I to judge?

GIVE ME THAT GODDAMN HAIRDO
GIVE ME THAT GODDAMN HAIRDO

Patti Smith: Songs have predispositions and parallel needs.
Srinivasa Ramanujan: To live another life, thought for thought, is always on my mind. I'm possessed by it, though frankly it's a willed immersion.
Patti Smith: Like telescopic visions, torn and damaged by fate?
Srinivasa Ramanujan: Or woven into narratives, rendered atonally.

YOU SHORT-STOPPED ME,
YOU GODDAMN SON OF A BITCH.

I'LL PUT A FUCKIN' FORK
THROUGH YOUR HAND.

YOU SHORT-STOPPED ME,
YOU GODDAMN SON OF A BITCH.

I'LL PUT A FUCKIN' FORK
THROUGH YOUR HAND.

Words to live by
Words to live by

I'VE NOW COME TO WHERE I DREAD
THE WORDS INSIDE OF MY HEAD
BLARING AN ENDLESS SONG
DISTANT FAITH SO FAR GONE

ARROGANCE BLINDS THE EYE
DAZZLED BY A FIREFLY
HEAR THAT DISTANT
TRUMPET-CALL?
PRIDE GOETH BEFORE A FALL

PRIDE GOETH BEFORE A FALL

The Punk & Poets Show

A. G. Geiger Art Bookstore
2-6pm Sunday 1/28/18

Featuring Crying 4 Kafka (plus)
outside on the patio (2-4pm) &
The Window Literary Series
(inside the bookstore) 4-6pm.

Chinatown Los Angeles 502 Chung King Court
90012

An Anecdotal Profile in Harmonic Cadence

Ovid

The Americana Desolation Music Academy
Joshua Tree, California

My job, if indeed it is a job, is to make sure that all of these exalted literary images do not obscure the appeal of the quotidian. A song, is a song, is a song. There is nothing else to fear, no need to emphasize despair, certainly not to the exclusion of a burning vortex or a nocturnal yearning, and there's no need to occupy tranquil bedrooms of city planners or their counterparts either, those blustering, bullying plumbers and tug boat captains trailing each other in their bathrobes, adrift in a sea of reflection. We are all obliged to look askance at Amazonian emporiums and butcher shops, those backwards bourgeois traces of respectability, while confining ourselves to New Mexican red chili powder and mung beans, masticating each mouthful at least 27 times, but not more than 44 or less than 16. Sleeping in the afternoon is still excusable, excluding of course, disgruntled bank clerks, telephonic dispensaries, and their ilk.

Gesture is ultimately the decisive thing, the proverbial drama in a teapot, mundane but rarely overdone, an inquisition of the humdrum, minutely as it were, Bolan on a gong, Bolan on a gong. Do we really need the third degree? Might the second do? If the goal is to fully occupy leisure, why do we repeatedly take selfies when the accelerating daily correspondents have abandoned the mire of contentment? If not for the blizzard of tweets and telegrams, enraptured and entreating as they might be, it is still nonetheless worthwhile to ponder without preemptory dismissal the folk wisdom of D.H.T., crucial to our civil, or is it uncivil existence so as not to remain in a vacuum of indecision, both unheard and unexamined, when composing etudes anchored in truth.

Soon, hopefully, the uncommon rapture stirred by the uncommon nature will become second only to nature itself, if not simply commonplace in the extreme. Cry and cry yet again, 4 or against, those setbacks now set adrift without accommodation, escaping the reckless confines and entanglements of inertia and deep dismay, secret shames finally disclosed and repackaged, and then transcribed by DNA electrophoresis in Morse code.

Though I want to have the feeling that you turn to me in need, with everything as it were, nothing, not the slightest thing escapes my purview, or is it my worldview, either way you never seem to reply, glued as you are to your cell phone and pocket calculator, figuring out this thing or that. Why can't I help? Why can't I break through these adamantine chains of perplexing sentences and grimaces on the sly?

To survive as a composer I can't live in resentments and revulsions that culminate in wrenchingly monastic repertoires of Liszt and Little Richard, the poets of self-entombment. I need the highways and byways of random firings of thoughts and feelings, grounded in historical truths or near-truths, to feed the flames of imagination, whole notes I call them, without taking leave of senseless writings on the surface of misunderstanding.

YOU ARE NOTHING BUT A PROFESSIONAL FUCK-UP. A PROFESSIONAL FUCK-UP.

YOU ARE NOTHING BUT A PROFESSIONAL FUCK-UP. A PROFESSIONAL FUCK-UP.

Swords to live by
Swords to live by

Robert Johnson: Dear Elizabeth: my song, *Cross Road Blues* is done, I guess. At least Don Law came to San Antonio to record it, though there was a delay, a ruthless detachment if you ask me, that continued through 2 aborted recording sessions, and countless other engagements, while I was working for pennies strumming on a sidewalk, a debasing ritual though it certainly helped in the sustenance department. Otherwise this has been a quiet Fall, composing and working on licks and finger picks. As far as gossip is concerned, I don't have much, except the conjugal shenanigans of Frankie and Johnny, who are still sweethearts. I do believe she has a hell of a temper.

Elizabeth Bishop: Dearest Bob: I listened to that scratchy recording you sent me previously of *Cross Road Blues*. It is truly fine. It is perhaps one of your best songs, though the other songs are good in an old kind of way, and for that matter, the new songs are good in a new kind of way. Altogether they are (the new songs) solid, real, intensely engaging, honest – and very interesting metrically. I think you should feel very proud of the whole effect. With lots of love as always…

Robert Johnson: Dearest Elizabeth: Many thanks for your comments. I feel that I write songs only for you and Lucille. I was just up in Arkansas, strumming and singin', displaying my ardent and contrarian spirit as best I can, feeling oddly estranged from my audience. I felt like a mastodon entertaining lizards. I'm hoping to reform them. Clapping hands and moving their feet would help.

Elizabeth Bishop: Dearest Bob: Fingers crossed. The gift btw went off to Eleanor. I feel that it's a poor match. Patrick is a persistent philanderer and a dissipated writer, distinguished in bookish circles but stymied on the page. Not an atypical affliction, but troubling nonetheless. My soft "hospital" buzzer tells me it's now dinnertime. The stars are huge and there is a deep yellow one. With much love.

I SPENT MORE MONEY ON TAXIS
THAN YOUR FAMILY EVER DID.

I SPENT MORE MONEY ON TAXIDERMY
THAN YOUR FAMILY EVER DID.

I SPENT MORE MONEY ON TOXICITY
THAN YOUR FAMILY EVER DID.

I SPENT MORE MONEY ON TOXIC
SHOCK THAN YOUR FAMILY EVER DID.

The American Scholar

Otis Redding, Ph.D.
Professor of History
University of California, Berkeley

Another sign of our times, also marked by an analogous political movement, is the new importance given to the single person. Everything that tends to insulate the individual—convictions too often erased by ambivalence for example, even when ostensibly steeped in minutiae – invariably disappear. I certainly don't mean revisionary posturing, those unmediated seizures of impulse torn from imaginary indiscretions that are quickly cobbled together by words built upon grave mumblings and comedowns either. What I had in mind instead was something that Bailyn once conveyed to me. *The American Revolution was not the over throw of the existing social order but the preservation of liberty*. What I'm now looking for is someone, anyone, who has strength of conviction to strive for truth. That person must have the ability to ingest all of the contributions of the past and all the hopes of the future. He or she must be a compendium of knowledge, a conservatory of music and an orchestra without imitation. We have listened too long to the courtly muses of Europe whereby American Scholars are purportedly timid, imitative, and tame. We need to walk on our own feet; work with our own hands; speak our own minds. A nation of American Scholars will then be born, inspired by the Divine Soul of Liberty, while ignoring the vestigial rustlings of outdated literary tinsels from across the Atlantic, those politicized harlequins of yesteryear. We need American scholars with verve and amplitude, with elevated riffs and American street vernacular, emboldened enough to get down on their knees, on stages throughout the land, to shout, and shout, and shout even more, until their words are barely audible, whispering, just whispering: try a little tenderness.

He's A Loser

by
Johnny and the Moondogs

He's a loser
He's a loser
He hides more than he shows.

Of all the vituperative harm he's cast,
Confused vicissitudes, broached and abashed.
Moving in a world with bitterness and blame,
Never knowing his Christian name.

He's a loser.
He baffles those who're near.
He's a loser.
He's not what he appears.

Although he laughs and acts the clown,
Executions nonetheless still abound.
Reigning bellows from a sigh,
Moral carnage to decry.

He's a loser.
He baffles those who are near.
He's a loser.
He's not what he appears.

What have I done to deserve this fate?
Muffled hope never crossing my gait.
Bedlam vexes unfettered and torn,
Sedatives, oboes, and French horns.

He's a loser
He baffles those who are near.
He's a loser
He's not what he appears.

STEP RIGHT UP
AND SEE THE MAN
HANGING ON A STRING
FROM A DISTANT HAND

HE LOOKS LIKE YOU
AND HE LOOKS LIKE ME
FLEET FOOTED WOODEN
PRODIGY

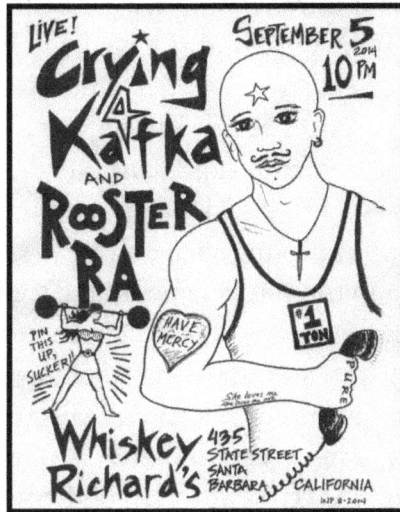

DON'T BE FOOLED
HE'S STILL ALIVE
EVEN A PUPPET HAS
BURNING DESIRES

THE CIRCUS IS ALL OF US
A WORLD OF IT'S OWN
SO VERY STRANGE
AND SO CLOSE TO HOME

A Plea for Admiral Harriet Tubman

Erika Blair
The Americana Desolation Music Academy
Joshua Tree, California

I trust that you will pardon me for being here. I do not wish to force **THIS MONTAGE** of thoughts upon you, but I feel compelled and estranged myself. The little that I know of Admiral Harriet Tubman should suffice. I will **NOT** fain, deign or Mary Jane to correct any misunderstandings, ruptures or discord. It will cost us **NOTHING** to be just and nothing to be true. The cravings, demands, and sentimental wastelands, lavished with adagio and punk rock bands, peering peevishly at literary grand dames, who lounge listlessly in **WONDERLAND** are made manifest in the voices of poets and the weavers of tales.

Harriet was born a slave in Dorchester County, Maryland. She escaped after seeing the melancholies and grievances, the miscreants and tortured chants, embellished with bitonality and confidantes in a resurrection dance. When the troubles began in Kansas land, **SHE** went to strengthen the party, as best she can, with the weapons she had at hand. This perhaps you know already. You already know this perhaps.

She was an old-fashioned woman in her devotion to the Constitution. She despised slavery and **SHE**, the singular she, was slavery's most formidable foe. Fraudulent writers, sermonizers in the abstract, Harriet repeatedly attacked and attacked.

There were of course other **DECENT** men and women, but she was more principled than all the rest. She was the best. She fought for the oppressed. Closeted, clandestine or transparently **WRONG**, Harriet would settle each score, an inflamed demigod primogenitor.

Why would *Billy the Kid*, or *El Salon Mexico* for that matter, condescend to being everyday disputations of American composition, abjuring to adherents of a strict classicism, void of a capacious or diverse ethnicity, to live side by side with critics and **COMMENTATORS** in castles made of jug bands? Slave-ships roam the open seas, with hatches and pens, time and again, everywhere and nowhere, except perhaps in chains, pains, and hurricanes, with rarely a murmur of indignation in congregations and destinations, that preach humility and futility, pious and righteous for all to see, sardonic **BUTCHERS** wed to the third degree.

Politicians assert that the only proper way to eliminate slavery is *the quiet diffusion of the sentiments of humanity*. Bodies of dead slaves cast overboard, last judgments feigned or ignored, casting pearls for the ascension of our lord. A *diffusion* of **HUMANITY?** Polyptychs of insanity. Tecumseh will eventually have his say, non-sequiturs and half tones in a passion play.

All is quiet at Harper's Ferry? Self-denying legislators and quixotically deluded knights in white sheets alienated from the foundations of liberty, striving Johnny come haters seizing humans in landscapes and lore, anchored in vanities of self-invention. A fulcrum of weights, bars, and **CHAINS** building cathedrals and penitentiaries out of blood and tears, for years and years, kept immaculately apart from bonnets and parasols, mint juleps and drawls, plantations and masked balls, and agencies for **TYRANTS** basking in lives unlived.

The only government that I recognize is a power that establishes justice. Not pretenders to the throne, Christians crucifying Christ, millions for certain, the White man's burden, never contemplating fiercely individuated minds, outliers cultivating literary confluence and multiply rendered compositions, singled out for **DAMNATION** only because of the color of their skin. When a government condemns a conscientious black woman, it's crumbling towards its own dissolution. Freedom is an immersion, a rare confluence linking need and achievement, acutely displayed and honorably arrayed, in the lives we live. *The Apotheosis of Liberty, The Ninth Amendment of Equity*, J.S. Mill on ecstasy, sonatas for infinity. Principles intricately crafted as recondite procreative fires, manifested in the internal morphological permutations of humanity. Though I have raised these principles in the condemnation of slavery, they are by no means limited to regrettable swaths of American history, privileged hermeneutical keys.

Why waste these **PRINCIPLES** on artifice and common denominators, as low as low can be, to feed the idols of commercialism and the vanities of absolutism? Are we truly limited to calculated gambits devised and purloined on pulpits accented by TR-808? Whatever happened to iconoclasts, uniquely possessed by the fire of imagination, in secret laboratories of the mind, smelting new aesthetics, infused **SOUNDS** and poetics.

Eminem, O Eminem, wherefore art thou Eminem? Deny thy father and refuse thy name. Listening to ambient cultures change, the times they are a changin' and a changin' again, veiled **INFLECTIONS** so inclined, unacquainted with the risks and uncompromised, hard-headed and aslant, refusing to dance to the paradoxes of chance, metronomes and gilded romance, intruders of ingratiating chants on *Desolation Row* I now surmise.

Perhaps I'm mistaken, missing the point, atonal as it were *Wozzeck* and the Berg. Academic it seems, reversing a theme, transforming an act. Rivalries come and rivalries go, uniformly grim to some at least, the untutored ears of cultural police. Why not redemptive radiance instead, music for thinking and startling too, melancholy textures welcomed at last, holding hands loud and fast, elusive melodies in thrall at the gate, conjured and shifting on interstates, perils and metaphors recreate, as disquisitions are given weight.

Every sovereign artist is obliged to be, an empire of one, an actuality, the shackled self, the muffled voice, **FREEDOM** only lives in the act of choice. It's the opportunity for choice that cultivates the voice, Harriet said, again and again. Chains, barriers, and obstacles built-in, are no less corrosive outside or within.

SECRETS HIDDEN WELL
WEARY INFIDELS
PITY SPREAD ON THICK
MORPHINE AND THE FIX
BUDDHA HOOKED ON METH
CLOWNS THAT QUOTE MACBETH
SPIRIT HANDED DOWN
SAINT AND HIS CROWN

FUCK MOM, FUCK DAD
FUCK ALL THE MEMORIES
I NEVER HAD

Thomas A. Dorsey: Dearest Elizabeth: Pleasant to have my record done. I feel like I can relax into joyous dissipation, i.e. playing the piano, seeing people. I've been reading Reinhold Niebuhr, *The Nature and Destiny of Man*. Spent some time in Georgia, staying with cousins, going to church. Chicago's a pleasant place, but there's so much gentrification and noise. The commercialism of it all has taken a toll on me. I often want to get away, perhaps for a year or two. I'm thinking the South, maybe even New Orleans. Brazil would be nice. I'd especially love to see you again. Do you think that some little gospel performance could be gotten for me that would pay my way? Love, Tom

p.s. those gospel recordings have finally arrived.

Elizabeth Bishop: Dearest Tom: Your photograph – the curly-headed one with the mysterious eyes has just come back from the framers. *Simply framed Tom*, as Marianne would say. Just a little cedar or cypress, whichever it is that the termites won't eat, and I've just waxed you with my own hands.

Mahalia Jackson's interpretation of your song *Peace in the Valley* really struck a chord (no pun intended). What a magnificent voice. I'm so pleased that she will also be recording *I'm Going to Live the Life I Sing about in my Song*. She'll do it justice.

At the end of the week I'm off to Cabo Frio for ten days or so. I hope to do some fishing. A friend has a very nice house there and a much too deluxe fishing boat, too.

I'm burbling like my poor dear Aunt Maud.

With Love, Elizabeth

Thomas A. Dorsey: Dearest Elizabeth: I'll write you a real letter in a few days, but this is just to ask a favor. How would you feel about writing a blurb for my new gospel album? It would be the only one I'd use and of course should be written any way that pleased you and seemed natural. I know how well you like my stuff, or hope I do; however, these things are sometimes awkward. I've also decided to dedicate *Never Turn Back* to you. Perhaps a blurb migthn't be the right thing after all. Anyway, think it over. Lotta Love, Tom

Elizabeth Bishop: Dear Tom: I am sorry this has taken me so many days. I hope you can use this blurb, or some of it. Do what you want with it, change the order around or use whatever sentences you want to, etc. The image of the dotted note may not say as much to you as it does to me but Joni likes it and urged me to send it along too. Of course there is lots more to be said! If it's too late I'll understand.

Much love, Elizabeth.

FUCK EM ALL IS WHAT I SAY
FUCK EM EVERY SINGLE DAY
FUCK THE WAY THEY
FUCK US OVER
FUCK THE SYSTEM THAT
GIVES EM COVER
FUCK TO STAND UP TO THIS SHIT
FUCK THE THANKLESS
HYPOCRITES
FUCK'S A WORD THAT
SAYS IT BEST
FUCK IS RAGE, FUCK IS JEST

MOTHER, FATHER

MOTHER, FATHER

7 Pool Players at
Frazer and the Golden Bough

by
Brooklyn Faire

We real cool

The Impossibility of Death in the Mind of Someone Living

We left school

Fabled advents of literary subversions

We lurk late

Cadres of defections and insurrections

We strike straight

Banality, Banality, and Banality Some More

We sing sin

Mezzo Clowns Clowning Around

Again and Again

Dull, mediocre, and constrained

Carryin' tunes

Now forgettable and pained

We die soon

We die soon

We die soon

In one form or another - however intended,
Negating the living, like figures in a shrine,
Pinnacles and exaltations hereby remembered
Halos and halos of 21st century crimes.

Where is Gabritschevsky?
Gabritschevsky I ask?
Incoherent and enraptured
Out of step with his class.
Abandoned in form
Abandoned in grace
Revering his progenitors
And plumbing his brains.

Plumbing his brains
Plumbing his brains

crying 4 kafka
the grownups
and more..

free
21+

c4k

BoHenry's
Saturday 6/3 @ 9pm.
1431 San Andres St. Santa Barbara, CA

WHERE THE HELL WERE YOU?
WEREN'T YOU TOLD TO PICK ME UP
AT 8 O'CLOCK?

WEREN'T YOU TOLD TO PICK ME UP
AT 8 O'CLOCK?

WHAT DO YOU MEAN
YOU FORGOT?

YOU GOD DAMNED LYING
SON OF A GUN.

WHERE THE HELL WERE YOU?

WEREN'T YOU TOLD TO PICK ME UP
AT 8 O'CLOCK?

WEREN'T YOU TOLD TO PICK ME UP
AT 8 O'CLOCK?

WHAT DO YOU MEAN
YOU FORGOT?

YOU GOD DAMNED LYING SON OF
A GUN.

I NEED A CELEBRATION
I NEED SOME INSPIRATION
I WANT TO FEEL INTENSE
I WANT MAGNIFICENCE

NO ONE EXACTLY KNOWS
WHERE TO GO
STEPS ARE NEVER CLEAR
FOOTPRINTS DISAPPEAR

A Treatise on Human Recording

Paul du Gre, Ph.D.
Professor of Engineering
California Institute of Technology

BOOK 1: Of the Origin of Music

Four Saints and Their Cousins was valued for its variegated intonations herding random sounds into a neo-classical composition. Oddly enough people called it Americana music. When I met Virgil, he was working with Orson Welles. Virgil complained *I need more voodoo. More voodoo I need.* Then he wrote his own violently percussive composition *Petticoat Injunction*, a speculative thesis cluttered with rivalry and hostile acts.

I started recording him shortly thereafter. We used the old Palomar Ballroom on Vermont. Dorsey, Miller, Artie Shaw all played there. It was a love affair, passionately declared and unavoidably compelled, acoustically that is. The cutting lathe was nearby, the inscription codified, and into the master cylinder it did rise, as required, as required. A venerated monument loomed unforgivingly, it seemed to me.

I didn't record that much during the World War II years or the fifties for that matter. It was still the age of form, when form, even when abandoned, was there to be abandoned, and abandoned again. The hard practice of virtuosity and those undiscovered metrics of rubato collapsing into a mock heritage of musical forms and pipsqueak epiphanies was the inevitable cacophony of drivel that invaded the world of music.

Wagner was still the rage. Rings on his hand, venom in his mouth, bolstered by fabricated culpability, the destruction of nature, pointing at fake showers, which I've seem myself, at Dachau no less, spewing poison and poison and poison again. I don't give a shit about a man or his legacy that aides and abets mass murder, a social worker for the damned, T.S. Eliot and Ezra Pound hand in hand, in a promised land of homogeneity.

It was for these reasons and more that I gave up recording entirely until the 1960s, the Byrds and the Doors, Sam Cooke and Bobby Fuller Four. I was obsessed and restored by gadgets galore and immersed in sound while indefatigably collecting Notes and certified checks.

Then came Doe, so capsized and perplexed, the tribal animosities, and of course the sex, mudslides and tornadoes, pain and remorse, contradictions and fairy tales, which Exene distorts, the dizzying keys, a Niagaran deluge, a thesis renowned, a behemoth consumed.

PCH
MALIBU
SUN IS BRIGHT
SKY IS BLUE

JAMES CAIN
RINGS TWICE
HUXLEY
ROLLS DICE

MORRISON
AND MCQUINN
TRADING SHOTS
DIDION

MISFIT
ANARCHIST

SO, SO, SO LA

HOLLYWOOD
ON THE MIND

BAD RELIGION
FAMOUS SIGN

DIEBENKORN
LOVE-LORN
DOING COKE
BEYOND BAROQUE

BOULEVARD
PROZAC DREAMS

GOVENOR
MOON-BEAM

OVER-SEXED
WHAT'S NEXT

SO, SO, SO LA

Do what one is told
Do what one is told
Do what one is told
Do what one is tolled

Confession

by
Agostin Saint-Germain

1. You are mighty, mighty you are, Mater my Mater. To be praised and embraced with a powerful voice I do rejoice: great is your goodness, and of your vision there can be no reckoning.

2. Please grant me, Mater, to understand better, your prophetic commands, the law of your lands. The friends we keep, the mates we reap, the Hoochie Coochie men from Mozambique. I must learn from this instruction.

3. Mater my Mater I must now confess that I am at a loss and I cannot guess, oh why, oh why, has the King proclaimed that I am a fuck-up to be defamed, a denigrated technocrat without a name, a professional fuck-up and I'm to blame.

4. Has the die been cast? I'm only seven years old.

5. My child. Though you speak urgently and endlessly to your Mater, there are things, magical things that you cannot as yet understand. These wholehearted preoccupations and aural syncopations, standing in prayer before me, conjuring your thoughts and turmoil, bruises and snake oils, to question the thrashings you have received at the hands of the King, do not concern me in any way or form. Nice is not what Kings are meant to be. The King has many responsibilities that a child, so wicked and so wild, could never comprehend. That is the province, for an elementary conscience. The King, besides, is not as bad as you say. Please leave now and go away. Find friends with whom to play. Come again, some other day, perhaps in May. August might do, the eighth or ninth, for instance.

Shut down at the Roxy,
wardrobe malfunction.

The lion, the witch,
the petticoat junction.

Shut down at the Roxy,
pasty gone awry.

The lion, the witch,
will indemnify.

The lion, the witch,
will indemnify.

Brand-on T-Bone: Though we construct venerated monuments to classicism that loom unforgivingly, must we conform to inflated rhetoric and sonorities, testamentary accessories without a thump?

Maria Callas: Sobbing renditions and reigning thunders are nothing more than mystical hazes. Librettos and stilettos are civilized pandemics. To hell with reveries and melancholic jigsaws of allusions. I stand behind the notes, *I puratani, I puratani,* that is.

Brand-on T-Bone: Touché. The portentously performed is no less a monument to commercialism than any other jingle that is shamelessly promoted to the hoi polloi.

Maria Callas: Those timid couplets and quatrains, disguised in the tics of conductor tricks, awash in magnificently drawn costumes and sets. Give me liberty, or give me death.

**KIERKEGAARD FEARED THE MOST
CROWDED HOUSE STACKED WITH GHOSTS
TIED HIS HEART TO THE WHIPPING POST
CRYING 4 KAFKA TONIGHT**

**NIETZSCHE WAS A SUPERMAN
LOCKED INSIDE A PRISON VAN
BULLET HOLES IN HIS HAND
CRYING 4 KAFKA TONIGHT**

**_WORLD ORDER IS A LIE
GOD IS DEAD AND WE SURVIVE
CAN'T EXPLAIN WHY WE DIE
READING KAFKA AS WE CRY_**

Existentialism is a Musical Idiom:
The Crying 4 Kafka Oeuvre

Jean-Paul Sartre
Café de Flore
Paris, France
(translated from the French by Ursula Del Aguila)

My purpose here is to offer a defense of a unique musical idiom, an empire stretched across the imagination of a savant. *Qu'est-ce que c'est.*

Crying 4 Kafka has been reproached as an invitation to dwell in despair, for souls who inhabit the fringe of nowhere. People like you and I know otherwise. We eschew ideologies and defunct mythologies when faced with uncertainty and the parables of the unknown. If every solution were barred, one would have to regard any action as entirely ineffective, except perhaps a contemplative and thoroughly bourgeois philosophy. This is, especially, the reproach made by the Commercialists about Crying 4 Kafka's forays into the unexplained.

From another quarter Crying 4 Kafka is admonished for having underlined all that is ignominious in the human situation, or for depicting what is mean, sordid and base thereby neglecting charm and beauty and the brighter side of human nature. Others reproach Crying 4 Kafka for failing to account for the solidarity of humankind or considering humans in repose. This, say the Commercialists, is because Crying 4 Kafka bases its doctrine upon pure subjectivity, making it impossible to regain cohesion and banality.

From the Christian side, Crying 4 Kafka is condemned as an entity that denies reality, presumably because it ignores the commandments of Bauhaus and the quatrains of Thomas Paine, as if nothing remains upon the brain, but that which is strictly voluntary.

It is to these various reproaches that I shall endeavor to reply, which is why I have entitled this brief exposition *Existentialism is a Musical Idiom: The Crying 4 Kafka Oeuvre*. Many may be surprised I mention a musical idiom, as if somehow I have succumbed to the deep voids of a proliferating cosmos.

I shall begin by saying that existentialism, certainly in my use of the word, is a doctrine of possibility, of exhalation and visceral sensation, a doctrine that affirms truth and human subjectivity. The essential charge laid against Crying 4 Kafka is, of course, the over-emphasis upon the evil side of human life. I have been told of a young woman, a doctor no less, who in moments of frustration will swear and then excuses herself by exclaiming, "I am a devotee of Crying 4 Kafka, oh my, oh my!" It now appears that inexplicable rage, dense or assuaged, is being identified with Crying 4 Kafka. Commercialists and Algerian engineers flock in troves to *No Country for Old Men*, yet are ironically repelled by the parables of *Ain't Always Paradise*.

CRYING 4 KAFKA

4/13/18

10PM FREE

THE DOUBLE DOWN SALOON
4640 PARADISE RD. LAS VEGAS, NV.

What could be more disillusioning than common sayings and preyings quoted for their mindless effect, whereby back peddling is preferred to uttering skepticism or dismay. Any action not in accordance with some tradition is mere romanticism or bolshevism. Why then must necklaces of Gordian knots, unadorned and obsessed, be put in place to restrain Crying 4 Kafka, and pulling plugs no less?

It is the Commercialists, gesticulating to the deities of marketing and greed, who complain that the music is too repugnant and unrestrained. Indeed, their excessive protests make me suspect that what is annoying to them is not so much the pessimism, but Crying 4 Kafka's humor and grace. Celebrating the parameters of choice, fundamental to liberty and humanity, is existentialism of the first order.

WHAT THE HELL ARE YOU TALKING ABOUT?
YOU FORGOT?
YOU GOD DAMNED FOOL!
WHAT DO YOU MEAN YOU FORGOT?

WHAT THE HELL ARE YOU TALKING ABOUT?
YOU FORGOT?
YOU GOD DAMNED FOOL!
WHAT DO YOU MEAN YOU FORGOT?

WORLD ORDER IS A LIE
GOD IS DEAD AND WE SURVIVE
CAN'T EXPLAIN WHY WE DIE
CRYING 4 KAFKA AS WE DIE
CRYING 4 KAFKA AS WE DIE
DADA DA DA DA, DADA DA DA DA
DADA DA DA DA. DAAAAA

Warden William Lewis:
Cruelties of Prison Life in Muddling Waters

Oscar Wilde
(Formerly Prisoner Number C33)
May 27, 1897, France

Warden Bill, Governor of Muddling Waters, is a man of gentle and humane character, greatly liked and respected by all prisoners. He was appointed last July. Though he cannot alter the rules of the prison system, implausibly conceived petty circumscriptions, he has altered the spirit in which his predecessor performed them. The system is of course beyond his reach. I have no doubt however that he sees injustice, stupidity, and morbid morbidity, though I have no real knowledge of his views of these operatic proceedings. I merely judge him by the change he brought about. Under his predecessor the system was carried out with harshness and perfidies.

I remain your obedient servant, *O.W.*

MANIFESTO 2.0

Crying 4 Kafka is a distant unregretted noise that eschews befuddled mysticism and declamatory strumming and humming and other habit-forming drugs that pander and meander to mainstream markets contaminated with pop culture and other vapid musings of superficial esteem.

STRANGE HOW THE SOUND OF A MADMAN
STOLE THIS SONG

STRANGE HOW THE SOUND OF A MADMAN
KILLED THIS SONG

STRANGE HOW THE SOUND OF A MADMAN
SPEAKS WHAT WE KNOW AND KNOW AND
KNOW AND KNOW

A MADMAN *SINGS* GREAT LOVE FROM
LITTLE THINGS MAY GROW AND
GROW AND GROW AND GROW

A MADMAN BURIED HIS HEART
SHATTERED IN A TRAGIC SONG
A MADMAN'S WISDOM LIVES
HIDDEN AWAY, WHERE IT BELONGS

A MADMAN SPEAKS
WHAT WE'RE AFRAID TO THINK
A MADMAN WRITES
IN A DISAPPEARING INK

A MADMAN WRITES
IN A DISAPPEARING INK

A MADMAN WRITES
IN A DISAPPEARING INK

GOD DAMN BULLSHIT ANSWER.

STARTING RIGHT NOW YOU ARE
FORGETTING THAT GOD DAMN CAR.

YOU GOD DAMN FOOL.

I'LL GIVE YOU SOMETHING
TO FORGET.

GOD DAMN BULLSHIT ANSWER.

STARTING RIGHT NOW YOU ARE
FORGETTING THAT GOD DAMN CAR.

YOU GOD DAMN FOOL.

I'LL GIVE YOU SOMETHING TO FORGET.

Letters to a Young Poet

by

Karl Popper

Your letter arrived just a few days ago and I wanted to thank you for the great confidence you have placed in me. I cannot however discuss your verses, for any attempt at criticism, which is fundamental to the way I think, would be act of futility. Nothing touches a work of Art or Science as much as criticism. Art and Science are not so manageable as people would have us believe; most experiences are insouciant sensations happening randomly in spaces, where words rarely enter, or are dismissed as mysterious dissenters in transitory dreams.

I must now tell you that your verses have no style of their own. They do however have hidden beginnings of something personal. I feel this most clearly in the last poem, *Brain Waste Yields Database Gold* that succeeds in melody and in the lovely poem *Assembling the Brain from Deep Within*. These poems are still not yet anything in themselves.

You have asked me whether your verses are any good. You have asked others as well. You send them to magazines and are upset with editors and predators that reject your work. Now (since you have said you want my advice) please take the following seven suggestions to heart. They will help you refrain from turning self-disclosure into satire, and indecencies into bonfires.

1) Art and Science begin and end with problems.

2) See new problems where none are thought to exist, and find new ways of solving those problems.

3) The strength of themes, dreams and theories, so fundamental to the Arts and Sciences, is measured by how well they withstand attempts to *falsify* them.

4) Art and Science are *not* simply the accumulation of observations or experiments. The Arts and Sciences are instead a Darwinian struggle for the survival of better themes, dreams, and theories.

5) Finding themes, dreams and theories that are better approximations of the truth is the sole aim of the Arts and Sciences.

6) There are no categories, repertories or subject matters where Art and Science are concerned. There are only problems and the urge to solve them.

7) The sole method of the Arts and Sciences is *criticism*. The Arts and Sciences are different from myths and monoliths because they are open to criticism, and modifications in light of those critiques.

Steve Stewart: We live by rhyme. Not necessarily in the mainstream, but in many streams, progressive, antiquated and benign. Time obviously matters too, innuendo and accelerando. And let us not forget song, which is always on my mind, Georgia of course, whom I certainly endorse, and Lenya Lenya, though hard to define, is still divine, her voice of tin and ephemera.

Jean-Pierre Rampal: Tomasi once said that the heart of a symphony is the slow movement, the Largo, the whispers and vespers, the incessant begging for notes high on the violin. Then Bobby and I, of contemplative minds, flute and harpsichord intertwined, took the States by storm, over a bank of tremolos.

Steve Stewart: The long day of post-modernism continues. In the end, we become the person we impersonate.

Jean-Pierre Rampal: If one listens carefully, without distraction: *It was better before, before they voted for Whats-His-Name*, it's apparent that Shostakovich has been absorbed with confidence.

MASSACRE IS THE GOAL
RID THE EARTH OF LIVING SOULS
DEVIL HAD A MASTER PLAN
KILL THEM ALL, AS THEY RAN

TORTURE MAKES IT EVEN WORSE
ACTING ON THE DEVIL'S CURSE
BULLET HOLES, NOTHING NEW
GENOCIDE, ME AND YOU

*WHEN HATE BECOMES
COMMONPLACE
YOU NEED TO PROTECT
THE HUMAN RACE*

*WHEN HATE BECOMES
COMMONPLACE
YOU NEED TO PROTECT
THE HUMAN RACE*

The Hedgehog and the Fugue

Isaiah Berlin
Oxford University

There is a line among the stanzas of the English poet Auden that says: *The fugue is a complex contrapuntal manipulation of many things, but the hedgehog only exploits kings.* Musical scholars have differed about the correct interpretation of these conjured words, susceptibility to exaltations of image-drenched librettos for example, which may mean nothing more than that the fugue, for all its repetitions, is eclipsed by the hedgehog's orthodox digressions and monarchal compliances. But, taken figuratively, the words can be made to yield a sense in which they mark one of the deepest differences between classicists and dramatists, and perhaps human beings more generally.

For there exists a great chasm between those, on one side, who relate everything to an all-embracing, sometimes self-contradictory and incomplete, but nonetheless unitary musical vision of the principles of composition and performance, and, on the other side, those desolate composers who embrace a daringly scathing and assertively fecund musical idiom performed in relentless fury without, consciously or unconsciously, seeking to fit themselves into, or exclude themselves from, any hard and fast rules.

The first kind of musician belongs to the hedgehogs, the second to the fugues; and without insisting on a rigid classification, we may, without too much fear of contradiction, say that, in this sense, Beethoven belongs to the first category, Bowie to the second; Debussy, Ravel, Shostakovich, Prokofiev, Gershwin, Britten, Bernstein, Ives, and Messiaen, in varying degrees, are hedgehogs; The Dead Kennedys, Social Distortion, Bad Religion, The Clash, X, The Sex Pistols, Hüsker Dü, The Stooges, and The Velvet Underground are fugues.

Of course, like all over-simplified classifications of this type, the dichotomy becomes, if pressed, artificial, blurred and absurd. But if it is not an aid to serious criticism, neither should it be rejected as being too resplendent or merely superficial; like all distinctions that embody any degree of truth, it offers a point of view from which to look and compare, a starting-point for genuine musical investigation.

Extremes, curiously enough, often become their opposites. Schoenberg's scandal-making chords, composed in defiance of Wall Street's trivialized elitist impracticality, have now seeped into the riffs of *London Calling*. Despite appearances otherwise, music is borderless, and walls, no matter how turgid, are meant for climbing.

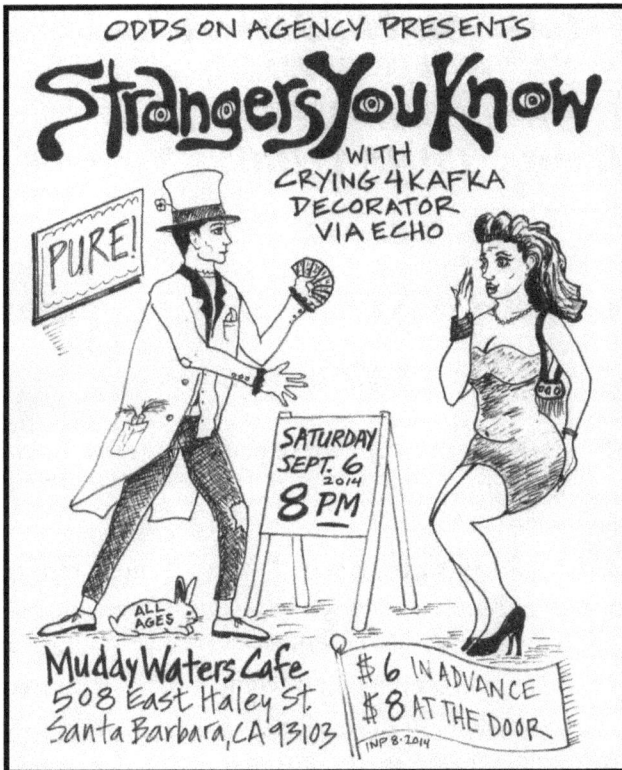

LOST MOMENTS NEVER RECOVERED
IMPRISONED WORDS TO A LOVER
EVERY MASK HIDES ANOTHER
DEEP REGRET I SOON DISCOVERED

THESE LESSONS HARD TO LEARN
IGNITE A FIRE THAT NEVER BURNED
LOST LOVE UNCONCERNED
ACROSS MY HEART NOW RETURNED

I HAD THE WORDS I WANTED TO SAY
THEN IT ALL SLIPPED AWAY
I EVEN KNEW WHAT TO DO
NEVER DID...COME THROUGH
NEVER DID...COME THROUGH

✶✶

Interlude

I thought I'd interrupt these proceedings to answer a few questions you might have.

1) Why did I take this approach? I'm not a biographer. I'm not a philosopher either. I'm a poet who is loath to embrace conventional form. In the construction of a band narrative, there's always a search for a deeper logic beyond the normative supplications.
2) What's the rationale for the poems? The lyrics scattered

throughout this book are illusory, pretending to be something they are not. The obscenities are traces of paternal wrath excavated for posterity. The putative authors are imagined, exigencies of the craft. The cadences, rhymes, and values are authentic.
3) Why write a book about a band that nobody knows? Why write a book about a band that everyone knows?
4) How do you feel when you listen to Crying 4 Kafka? Excited, intrigued, swept away.
5) What's the best story about this band? They don't give a shit about stories.

Erika Blair
Joshua Tree, California
2/2/18

****

Tsumi O Kokuhaku

by

Jun'ichirō Tanizaki

(Translated from the Japanese by James Baldwin)

We feel embarrassed (*hazukashii*) about contraceptives. We use methods that don't require speaking to a doctor. Women don't like gynecological exams. Condoms are available in vending machines.

Couples use body temperature to check for ovulation. It shares responsibility between man and woman.

Marriages used to be arranged. A go-between reduced the shame of courtship defeat. Rejection weighs heavily upon a family. We are prone to depression.

There is no word for love. We say *ski-desu* or *dai-ski-desu*; like and like a lot, respectively. I never told any of my six wives that I loved them. They wouldn't believe me. It would embarrass them.

Americans draw a heart. They put the names of lovers in the heart. We draw an umbrella. We put the names of lovers on each side of the shaft. We share an umbrella when it rains. It rains often in Kyoto.

We don't condemn pleasures of the flesh. We keep them in place. Savored but sacrificed to duty.

Insidious desires were my undoing. They brought shame to my family. *The Key, Some Prefer Nettles, Like Finding Love in a Vending Machine.*

Now we have two types of marriages: the go-between and mutual attraction. Love plays no part. We chose instead someone who would run a good home. A good home can last forever.

I was possessed, obsessed, and then proscribed. I'm a bad example. Do not follow the path I took.

We are shy people. We do not make marriage vows. We communicate with our eyes. *Ishin Den Shin.* One mind informs the opposite mind.

We don't say that we will be faithful. I have been *unfaithful.* People think that only husbands are unfaithful. That is not true.

Wives used to help husbands dress for visits to prostitutes. Wives would pay the bill for a prostitute if the bill were sent to the home. Not anymore.

CONSOLED MYSELF
EVERYDAY
LOVE BENDS
SO THEY SAY

SAW THE SIGN
EVERCLEAR
RESTLESS POET
DISAPPEARED

Bob Dylan: Dearest Elizabeth: Finally heard from Albert, whom I'll see in two or three days. Very cordial – *Some of these songs are especially good. I have a hunch that this album will be most successful.* He mailed two short letters – one three weeks old, the other one week.

I'd really like to come visit. I wonder if Albert could set something up at the University in Rio. I'm more suited to performing for students than singing for polite audiences.

I'm working with a guitar player, Mike. He's a shaman and capable of igniting the music, but I have to be cautious.

Joan is working on a new album. I like it - it's more poetic and doesn't rely upon so many tremolos.

Did I tell you that Phil and Jack both separated from their wives? They still see each other once a week. Maybe they'll go back, but that too fills one's soul with dolor.

I've been reading Wang Xiaobo. A strange novella about young lovers exiled in China. Lots of sex and endless confessions. James has been helping me read the Chinese.

My love to you and Lota, Bob

Elizabeth Bishop: Dearest Bob – I went to Rio to have a tooth pulled and while there saw the assistant to the Cultural Attaché who reproached me with: *You didn't tell me that Bob had performed* *in London!* So apparently, they have been doing a little research. Mr. Morris said that he's applying from his end but he seems a little uncertain as to his pull with the State Dept. And again, he said that the best and most certain way would be for Albert to make a direct application to the State Dept. It is called something like "Exchange of___?" persons? I'm going down to Rio this afternoon and shall ask again. Lota says we will exchange you for a ton of coffee.

I can't help but feel that Belle is making a great mistake – a fourth marriage at her age – but then, I'm afraid I've never understood Cat's appeal to my sex very well.

We have just been cleaning the living-room light furnace- deep bowl-shapes- because we had a short circuit last night and they all blew out. In each one we find about a half a peck of baked insects, moths, beetles, all sorts - completely dried-up and the color of old manuscripts.

Much love to you and your family, too. Elizabeth

Bob Dylan: My dearest Elizabeth. I've been meaning to write you a Confusion-like letter. I think the trip to Brazil had better wait another year. My therapy (three days a week with R. D. Laing) is doing great things. I have begun to hope that the creative knot inside of me will soon be unsnarled.

It has recently dawned upon me that my dust-cloud of scythes has been largely about trying to tell stories that don't collapse into idle banter. Some songs are more successful than others.

By the way, the black velvet jacket you sent me has just come through. It's lovely. I'll have Marianne take a Polaroid picture and I'll send it to you, unframed of course.

Love, Bob

Elizabeth Bishop: I have two letters here to answer, one a particularly nice one. Also, I'm going to write a blurb for your new album and send it shortly.

But Lota is going to Petrópolis *right now*, and I thought I'd like to get this much in the mail for you at least. I'll write either tonight or tomorrow morning. I've been spending a great deal of time listening to *Desolation Row.* I can't get it out of my mind.

I'd love to see you perform in Washington, D.C. Claire Booth-Luce is NOT coming here – but more later.

With Much Love, Elizabeth.

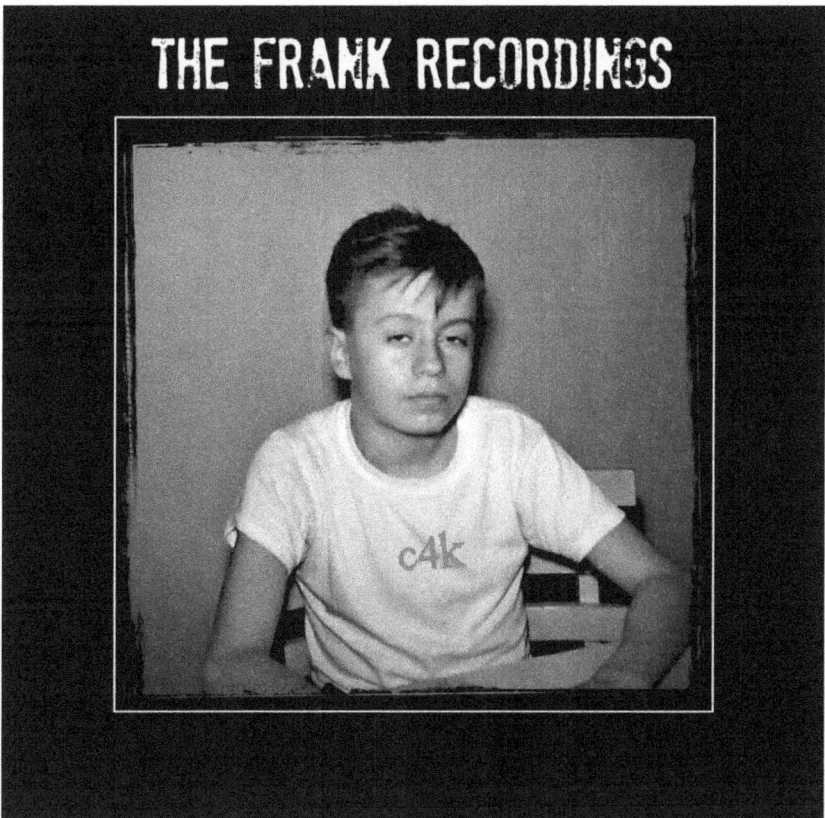

THE FRANK RECORDINGS

All of these jackoffs at the office
The rapist in the pool
Oh and the tragedies in the nurseries
Little kids packin' guns to school…
And sex kills everything
Sex kills…

(Joni Mitchell, *Sex Kills*, 1994, *Turbulent Indigo*)

SKATING ON ICE IN PARADISE
CAME SO CLOSE TO THE TRUTH
AFRAID TO TELL THE INFIDEL
I MISS THE PROSTITUTE

UNCHAIN
VERITE

UNCHAIN
VERITE

UNCHAIN
VERITE

UNCHAIN
VERITE

The Origin of Composition in the Breakdown of the Quantum Mind

Greg Graffin, Ph.D.
Professor of Physics
Institute for Advanced Study
Princeton University

There's something subdued and bloodless about musical stirrings and blurrings that reminds me of Tin Pan Alley composers recollecting the joys of telephone booths and automated dining. Absorbed by recondite theorizing or scampering after newfangled hooks and crooks, so many contemporary composers fawn over music that is pointedly inaccessible to anybody except music executives high on coke and industry gossip. Those types embrace the doctrine of impersonality, preferring above all else to hitch their wagons to payola and facile contrivances, as if artistry was reducible to cash and pastiche, cisterns fixed upon the firmament of AM radio, a vanquished medium that once was magisterially dominated therein. Why do we even bother with exactingly allusive commercial hits that are an anathema to manifold ironies and inflections - or persist in the pursuit pleasurable ribbons of ennui - that are rarely composed of ingenuity and enchantment?

I have always assumed that functional design is something that can be easily comprehended by a composer and convincingly communicated to others. We don't need gimmicks or focus groups, impersonal and exportable, to concoct songs lured by unfamiliar absolutions and immobilized disjointed despair manufactured by the cultural dictators of conformity. *Seven Types of Continuity* is perhaps the best way to describe the music industry. Even the pretense of "new music" is nothing more than medieval theology in the absence of dissent, which is why so many of us resisted the glaze of orthodoxy in favor of punk rock music, a deconstructive torrent of metaphysical discord.

Which brings me to the work of A. Wendt. *Bach's thinking*, he said, *exhibited quantum coherence – in effect, Bach was a composing wave function. His compositions are best understood as a quantum decision-making process, or perhaps a quantum probability theory.*

I'm now thinking that it might useful to consider punk rock music from this vantage point. Rather than a joyous denouement consecrated to mosh pits and mayhem, perhaps it's worthwhile to also recognize the churning winds of subatomic storms, *Quantum Sorrow in D Minor*, for example. Within this inferno we may find clarification of what has been, and what might yet be.

MATTER OF FACT, NEVER STARTED A WAR
MATTER OF FACT, NEVER SETTLED A SCORE
MATTER OF FACT, NEVER FALSELY ACCUSED
MATTER OF FACT, NEVER SANG THE BLUES

NEVER RULED THE ROOST
NEVER ON THE LOOSE
NEVER CARRIED THE BALL
NEVER TOOK THE FALL

THIS IS IT, I WANT NO MORE
TWISTED RULES THAT I DEPLORE
BLESSING PEACE AND WAGING WAR
THIS IS IT, I WANT NO MORE

A Brief Exegesis on Rock n' Roll

Tim Cool-Man
Warsaw Banjo Band

Rock n' roll musicians, armed with their arrogant demeanors and adhesive addictions, leashed to the dreary fictions of commercial suck-cess and the tedious benedictions of hashtags and credit card debts. If indeed an innovative form should ever emerge, it quickly dissolves into rules and commandments, the mainstays of fashionistas and bandits, serving Gods of GREED and their faithful propagandists.

Break the rules. Break the rules.

DE DOMO Rules.

The forces of evil in a bozo nightmare
Ban all the music with a phony gas chamber
Cause one's got a weasel and the other's got a flag
One's on the pole, shove the other in a bag

(Beck, *Loser*, 1993, *Mellow Gold*)

I HAD A DREAM, THE ACCIDENT
FUCKING PEOPLE MAKE NO SENSE
BLACKENED WORLD, WHERE
RAGE PREVAILS
DESPERATION ON THE RAILS
SWELL OF MISERY AT NIGHT
DEAD END STREETS AND DYNAMITE
PARENTS SING A LULLABY
VOICES TREMBLING, BOMBS FLY BY

WHAT THE FUCK ARE YOU
DOING THERE
ON YOUR KNEES WITHOUT
A PRAYER?
WHAT THE FUCK ARE YOU
DOING THERE
ON YOUR KNEES OR DON'T YOU
CARE, AT ALL?

DO YOU, DO YOU, UNDERSTAND?
MONEY, MONEY, TAKE MY HAND

DO YOU, DO YOU, UNDERSTAND?
MONEY, MONEY, AIN'T LIFE GRAND?

RUN FRANK, RUN
RUN FRANK, RUN
RUN FRANK, RUN
RUN FRANK, RUN
RUN FRANK, RUN
RUN FRANK, RUN
RUN FRANK, RUN
RUN FRANK, RUN

Mando-Pop

by

Li Bai

(translated from the Chinese by Professor Keith Holyoak)

I'm idling alone in the deep counterminings of art where censorship is the mother of metaphors and insolent minotaurs. I have a constitutional necessity to compose songs without worrying about sanctions, in combination with an affinity for peculiar images that are guided by echolocation and ambidexterity. *The*

Saint of Fucked-up Karma, Humbled by the King of Porn and *Contemplating Whores Again* all roam a musical landscape that leaves nothing unobserved, operating as they do, under the logic of locution. Accumulated memories then feed the irony that mocks the plausibility of commercial integrity and trust. The temple of gold is the only throne upon which the Kings and Queens of Corporate America sit high and lifted up.

去和平

READ THE FLYER
HEARD THE CHANT
SUSPICIOUS MIND
INTOXICANT

DOOR AJAR
STARING THROUGH
SAID TO MYSELF
NOTHING LOOKED TRUE

EVERY JOURNEY HAS AN END
EVERY FOE SEEKS A FRIEND
EVERY WOUND WANTS TO MEND
EVERY VOW IS PRETEND

EVERY VOW IS PRETEND
CRY YAH NOA MORTAL LIEEEEEEEEEEE

Marc Bobro: The predicament is complex, the euphonium not-withstanding. The double bass is often double **TROUBLE** for truncated spirits of drollery. Nuance fortunately re-emerged in an essay by Wittgenstein that cleared away external fingering styles in anticipation of the next wave of percussion.

Spinoza: The world would be so much nicer if everyone would just shut up. **ABSTRUSE** mathematical taunting about free will would disappear, roundly excoriated by sedulously detached pundits of print. I say, and have said over and over again, *fuck free will and the metaphysics of self-determination.* Give me John Cage or give me death.

Marc Bobro: I used to go to Paris to listen to Foucault, a Corsican composer whose charm was manifested in automated metaphorical enigmas, the opera *Perovskites from all Angles*, for example. I'd also visit Henri Sauguet, another French **COMPOSER**, who populated his ballets with imagined characters from *Gimpel the Fool* and *Madame Bovary*.

Spinoza: Despite the sonic erasures that romp through contemplative transcendence and claw feverishly at sophistry and idolatry, we still can't control our feelings, but we can control our **EVALUATIONS** of those feelings. By doing so, we can then counteract the passions that control us, encoded as they are in mutely intrusive languages, and thus achieve some relief from their turmoil. *I must not think bad thoughts. I must not think bad thoughts.*

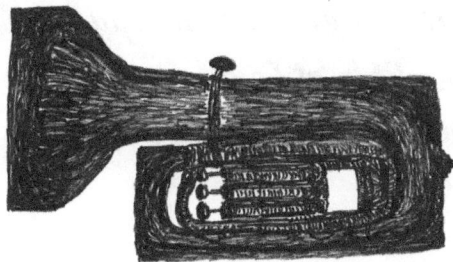

They Pulled the Plug at Reds
I Was Gonna Have Her Blow You Guys
They Pulled the Plug at Reds
  Hypocrisy in Fresh Supply

Rainbow Bridge

by
Hart Crane

How many dawns, chill from this rippling rest
Must inflame the ancient argument,
Ruminating on the harness of piety
Over the chained bay waters of Liberty—

Then, with inviolate curve, forsake our eyes
As voices reflect pulsings of the past
Sacred testimonies to be filed away;
—Commanding threads reflected and betrayed...

I think of compositions and panoramic sleights
With multiple beats toward a flashing scene
Never disclosed, but hastened to again,
Foretold in visions on mescaline.

And Thee, across the stage, silver paced
The nimbus of expectation fades
Implicitly at the margins of disguise,
Languishing in thy freedom it stayed

An ensemble of cello and flute
A sodomite speeds to thy parapets,
Tilting with exalting shrill notes dazzled,
Falling from a speechless minuet.

Stonewall, from girder into street noon leaks,
A rip-tooth of the sky's acetylene;
All afternoon the familiar derricks overturned...
Riddled omens erupt on Benzedrine.

THE SAINT OF FUCKED UP KARMA

a punk rock musical by CRYING 4 KAFKA

LIVE @ Center Stage Theater

**HOLY ROLLER, WITH A BOOK
IN HIS HANDS
I REMEMBER, THE SHOUT
OF COMMANDS
HOLY ROLLER, IN A CHORUS OF CONS
SINGING ABOUT KINGS
AND BABBLING ON**

HOLY ROLLER, KEEP AWAY
FROM MY SOUL
DEMI-GODS ON STILTS, WITH YOUR
JUDGEMENT PAROLE
HOLY ROLLER, PUT THE BARBS
IN THE WIRE
HIDIN' IN PULPITS, UNTIL
FREEDOM EXPIRES

THERE'S BLOOD IN THE RAIN
AND IT'S STARTED AGAIN
CROSSES ARE POINTED
AND EVERYONE'S SINNED
THEY'RE BURNING A PLACE
WHERE NOBODY ESCAPES
IT'S TIME FOR THE ONE WHO
DETERMINES...HIS OWN FATE

The Sacred and the Profane

Erika Blair
The Americana Desolation Music Academy
Joshua Tree, California

Evangelists trust the veracity and concrete particularities of their tomes, ad hoc contrivances notwithstanding. Scrutinizing evidence for absolute congruence between science and facts is rarely apparent. They prefer instead bewitched contraptions and oratory distractions.

The philosophers and sermonizers of self-illumination who march to the beat of irreversible drummers swaggering toward glorified moral destinies that began with romantic ambitions and always end with bloody pandemonium is yet another matter entirely. Their doctrines are nothing more than prideful tales, erected on rickety stilts, searching for golden challises and world domination, built upon the backs of ideological slaves and minions, while gilded clerics adorn themselves with red diamonds and matching Prada loafers.

Must Crying 4 Kafka be categorized as profane because it asserts that the liberty of conscience is fundamental to personal autonomy? *I didn't know I was a slave until I found out I couldn't do the things I wanted to do*, Frederick Douglas once said to me in Joshua Tree.

NIGHTS THAT I'M LONELY
KEEP ON HEARING IT FROM YOU
ALL THAT SHIT, THAT I DO
AND I AIN'T GOTTA CLUE

THE FACES THAT I LOVE
SO IMPRACTICAL
DAMNED THEATRICAL
AND YOU'RE DONE WITH IT ALL

HEY. I'M NOT SORRY
I DON'T FIT IN YOUR PLANS
HEY. IM NOT SORRY
I'M NOT YOUR KIND OF MAN

TOOK ME ASIDE, AND SHE SAID "ONE DAY KID,
I'M GONNA LET YOU CLIMB INSIDE."
TEACH YOU THE SECRETS OF THE LATE-NIGHT
ON A LATE-NIGHT HIGHWAY RIDE
MAN, SHE WAS STUNNING, JUST STANDING
THERE ALONE
"FRANK", SHE SAID, "I'LL BE YOUR BEST
DRESSED CHAPERONE."
DANCING AND SINGING FOR A HOME
AT COMMUTERS LIQUOR STORE

MISFITS
HYPOCRITES
FULL OF SHIT
JESUITS
MAKING BETS
NO REGRETS
SPINNING LIKE PIROUETTES
OSCAR WILDE
LOVE-CHILD
JACK SPICER RECONCILED
FREEDOM
DELIRIUM
PENDULUMS
AND SUGAR PLUMS

IT'S SODOMY, IT'S SODOMY, IT'S SODOMY
GIVE SODOMY A CHANCE

GIVE SODOMITES A CHANCE

Erika Blair
The Americana Desolation Music Academy
Joshua Tree, California

A fundamental right is a right that has been enshrined in the U.S. Constitution—the freedom of speech, for example. Fundamental rights also elicit judicial deference when conflict arises between an established liberty (e.g., speech) and governmental incursion (e.g., censorship).

The right to privacy however is not a fundamental right. Cobbled together in 1965, it was designed to protect married couples making contraceptive decisions in the privacy of their homes. Subsequently broadened and extended to unmarried heterosexual partnerships and their variegated intonations, the right to privacy nonetheless left sexual minorities out in the cold. That situation changed in 2003, when the U.S. Supreme Court finally acknowledged in *Lawrence v. Texas* that adult sexual minorities had privacy rights in the bedroom, too.

Lawrence did not create a fundamental right to sodomy—or any other sexual right, for that matter. Lawrence merely championed the benefits of emotionally durable and intimately incurable relationships. Gay marriage (*Obergefell v. Hodges*) extended this logic as a resilient symbol of equality. Sexual rights themselves, nonetheless, were held in abeyance, as if sexual identity were peripheral to the sexual choices made.

Privacy is not synonymous with sex. It's an allegorical door behind which people do *stuff*, often reduced to detritus and haphazardly defined and redefined over decades. The freedom to make sexual choices is instead the determinative right, not the lock on the door.

How can *real* sexual rights be assured? The answer is the Ninth Amendment: *The enumeration in the Constitution of certain rights shall not be construed to deny or disparage others retained by the people.* Without sex, there would be no people, and without people there would be no rights. Sexual rights are thus deeply rooted in the bedrock of the rights retained by the people, by the people, by the people.

Thomas Paine once declared, *A long habit of not thinking a thing wrong, gives it a superficial appearance of being right, and raises at first a formidable outcry in defense of custom.* This statement is true, no doubt, about sexual rights, too, customarily exercised through choice, the right to choose procreation being no less a right than choosing not to procreate.

Give Sodomites A Chance, Give Sodomites A Chance, **Give Sodomites A Chance.**

THE SAINT OF FUCKED-UP KARMA
CAME TO ME IN A DREAM
ANGEL IN A CROSSWALK
A LEGEND IN EXTREME
FIRE BROKE OUT WITHIN HIM
WHILE SHINING IN THE SUN
I'M GOING BLIND, HE SCREAMED
WALKING ON THE RUN

PUNK SONG no. 1

by

John Berryman

Haleakala crater I decided to climb today
Unappeasable I sulked away
Rebellious flight from inertia
The road was flooded
Scarcely buried a grievance yet
Decrying domesticity and riddles again

I pulled over to read a map
Johnny Lydon pulled over too
Spiky hair and silver teeth
He showed me the way
Deferred but not denied,
I took another path

A Chinese gravesite laden with beads
Taro patches remaining mute
Subterranean elixirs on a shelf
Overcast and humid too
Road to sugar bled a trail
Parsed and parsed in futility

A light rain started to drip
Restraint in the air
Waterfalls elude such tests
Enchantment and bitterness
Faithful mongrel bridges
Multiplicities so conspicuous.

TYRANTS AND TYRANNY
TYRANTS AND TYRANNY
CREATING RAGE & MISERY
CREATING RAGE & MISERY

Letter to My Father

by
Franz Kafka

Dearest Father,

You asked me recently why I claim to be afraid of you. I did not know, as usual, how to answer, partly for the very reason that I am afraid of you, and partly because an explanation of my fear would require more details than I could ever make coherent. And if I now try to answer in writing, it will still be nowhere near complete, because even in writing, my fear and its consequences, raise a barrier between us, and because the magnitude of material far exceeds my memory and my understanding.

The underlying issue seems very simple to you. You have worked very hard, sacrificed everything for your children, particularly me, and as a result I lived *like a lord*. I had complete freedom to study whatever I wanted, I knew where my next meal was coming from, and I therefore had no reason to worry about anything. For this you asked no gratitude.

Despite all of your efforts, what you claim that I would do instead was to hide away in my room, composing music, entertaining crazy friends and exploring eccentric ideas for songs. We never spoke openly, I never came with you to the synagogue, and I never seemed to have any sense of family. Though you say that I have never lifted a finger to help you, you are convinced that I will do all I can for perfect strangers.

If you were to summarize your resentment, the worst that you have ever done to me is to call me a *professional fuck-up*. If you believed that I needed extra motivation, your worst sin was to yell, *I'll have your ass suckin' sand!*

What exactly does that mean? *I'll have your ass suckin' sand.* I can't figure it out. Max can't either.

Franz

MY OL' MAN
HE SAID TO ME

"FRANK, YOU'RE GOIN', GOIN' TO SEE."

YOU WIN BIG
YOU LOSE IT ALL
YOU WAIT AND SEE

ALL I KNOW, IS WHAT I KNOW
ALL I SAY, WILL GO AWAY
EVERY THOUGHT, IS WRITTEN DOWN
EVERY WORD I'LL BETRAY

NOTHING SEEN, BELONGS TO ME
NOTHING HELD, WITHOUT CHAINS
NOTHING HERE WILL EVER STAY
EVERY WISH REMAINS THE SAME

DRUGS AND DRAMA
I OVERHEARD
QUEEN OF HEARTS IN A CAGE
DRUGS AND DRAMA
AT THE DOOR
NOTHING I'VE EVER SEEN BEFORE

POWDER HER FACE
POWDER HER FACE
POWDER HER FACE

Tom Ades's opera *Powder Her Face* was such a disgrace to the tidy paper chase of inertia. Mary Poppins entertaining descending minds poised to absorb the bracingly stale and commonplace but could never appeal to transcendent secrets of exterminating angels or their antediluvian counterparts. Fates and subversions beating endlessly to the shudder of tom-tom drums and Navajo chants, the strangeness of which is so inspiring to artists of solidity and precision. Wordsmiths of the observed, shaking tambourines and carrying parasols on holidays in May who cast astonishing bon mots, transfigured Christmas ornaments, and punk rock music into the drama of daily lives in the dismal hope of counterbalancing celebrity confessionals concocted by publicists working feverishly in *Edward Scissorhands* elastic PANTS.

**FUNNY HOW
SO INSANE
WE BECOME
WHAT REMAINS**

**GOTTA THINK
WHAT THIS MEANT
HALF-FORGOTTEN
TESTAMENT**

CRYING 4 BEAVER

STARRING
Crying
Kafka

AND

EVIL
BEAVER
NOTORIOUS
LA PUNK DUO

PLUS
SPECIAL
GUESTS

SATURDAY
FEB.
14

A VALENTINE NIGHT
EXTRAVAGANZA!

ALL
AGES

5 BUCKS
8 PM

PURE

MUDDY WATERS CAFE
508 E. HALEY SANTA BARBARA, CA
805·966·9328

IAN PUTNAM
1·2015

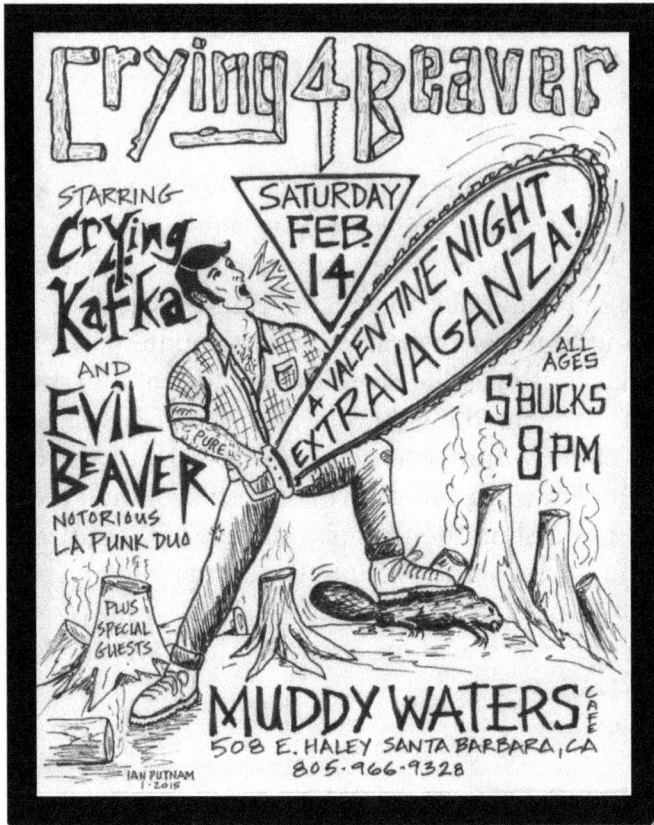

I CAN'T SEE
WHY WE CARE
WHAT'S BEEN DONE
BEYOND REPAIR

TRY AGAIN
HERE I COME
HIDE YOUR HEART
HIDE YOUR GUN

ME, ME, ME

Erika Blair
The Americana Desolation Music Academy
Joshua Tree, California

The great exposition of ME, ME, ME, and the incomprehension of skepticism and remorse has now collapsed into a discipline of trivia and tweets multiplying in hot pursuit of LIKES. No more conceptualization or debate, no cult of critique. Only a monolith of splitters, codified in texts, and enshrined in social media, where sound bite traffic engineers are feted and pursued by demagogues carrying gilded secrets and neon flasks.

I WAS DIFFERENT, OR SO YOU SAID
NOT ONE OF THE WHORES
YOU TOOK TO BED
IN A CASTLE, OR SO IT SEEMED
A GILDED CAGE, MISTAKEN QUEEN

Charles Olson: I want to show you what I call projective tunings. How I put them into certain laws and the possibilities of breathing in players who listen. The trochee's reprieve and the corrective make-believes delineate the minimalist roilings of Hüsker Dü.
Rick Ambrose: Lyrics make the song. I'm sick and tired of sentimental nostalgia for unrequited mayhem. What I prefer are self-indulgent yearnings for lust, hubris, and the syncopated excitement of bent strings and bowed guitars. Valéry's *Symphony for the Devil*, Jimmy Page's *Dazed and Confused*.
Charles Olson: A fight between grasshoppers is a joy to crows.

89

**ONE DAY, WHEN SHE GOT HOME,
SHE FOUND HER HUSBAND IN BED
WITH ANOTHER WOMAN,
SHE WENT INTO THE KITCHEN,
GOT A KNIFE,
WENT BACK INTO THE BEDROOM
AND...**

**SHE STABBED HIM, MOSES
SHE STABBED HIM, MOSES
SHE STABBED HIM, MOSES
SHE STABBED HIM, MOSES**

*The Sound Guy Pulled the Plug at Red Cove
and Walked Away.
Bryan put it back again.
The Sound Guy Pulled the Plug at Red Cove
and Walked Away.
Bryan stole his violin.*

Ian Putnam: Bitterly and blasphemously and mockingly unforgiving. What is it about this kind of music that makes it so irrepressibly articulate?

David Bowie: All of those songs are made of stardust channeled through a clannish cabal devoted to vindictive havoc and musical mayhem. *All the Young Dudes* owes its power to energy released by nuclear fusion at the core of that song. That very same reaction created the chemical elements of *Rebel Rebel* and *Heroes* - the building blocks that make up the world I inhabit.

Ian Putnam: So much music today is dull, self-deprecating, and submissive. The monotonous rhythms and perfunctory chords, while performers gesticulate slavishly to the Gods of conformity, the inextricable roller-coaster of catch phrases and slogans, never transfixed by the subliminal stages of pathos or uncertainty. Even the crack of a guitar solo is a distant memory, replaced instead by conventional narratives and supremely tender ministrations.

David Bowie: During a supernova, when a massive star explodes at the thin white duke of its life, the resulting high-energy environment scatters meteors across the universe.

Crying 4 Kafka

live @ stockmal

Toooo loud in LA on Halloween night.
Toooo loud in LA on Halloween night.
They called the cops.
THEY CALLED THE COPS.

Lose that band or you'll lose me
Lose that band or you'll lose me.

THE SOUND I REMEMBER
IS ECHOED IN A SONG
THE COMFORT THAT I SOUGHT
HAS COME NOW AND GONE

AS I LAY RESTLESS
IN AND OUT OF DREAMS
I'M HOLDING YOU CLOSELY
IT'S HARDER THAN IT SEEMS

PROMISES NEVER SPOKEN
HIDING IN THE HEART
FOR STANDING IN THE SHADOWS
AH. NEAR ENOUGH TO SPARK
NEAR ENOUGH TO SPARK

An Ode for Robin Finck

by
Giacomo Leopardi

In the valley, where the song
of the weary troubadour unfolds,
and when I sit and reflect upon
the illusions of fame and fortune,
I think of you and smile.

Whether you are the only one
of eternal wisdom
who refuses to conform
to the expectations of mortal life,
managing instead to live in spheres of accelerando,
foraging complex bursts of meaning
lovelier than the Sun,
I cannot say.

GUIDO DIDN'T WANT TO SEE NO BARS
PAID A FINE THE SIZE OF MARS
THEN IT WAS, FOREVER EVER MORE
CHECKBOOK – REVOLVING DOOR

LAWYER - HE - PULLS ME ASIDE
WE'RE BLEEDING MONEY, LEFT & RIGHT
NO MORE FINES – NO SLIDING-SCALE
DO HIS BIZ INSIDE THE JAIL

Letter to Mattia

Arturo Toscanini
Trento, Italy

Thank you for your kind comments and thoughtful questions. The composition of music is not simply the continuous dynamic recrystalization of sound during severe sonic deformation, but instead, it's more like an aural elastic constitutive law for sound waves. I remember working on this problem when I was at *La Scala* and then later with the *New York Philharmonic*. It's probably most evident in my *Essay for Orchestra*. The complete microinstructional evolution of my ideas was *Debussy's La Mer*.

I hope this explanation answers your question. I enjoyed your letter. *Ciao*, Arturo

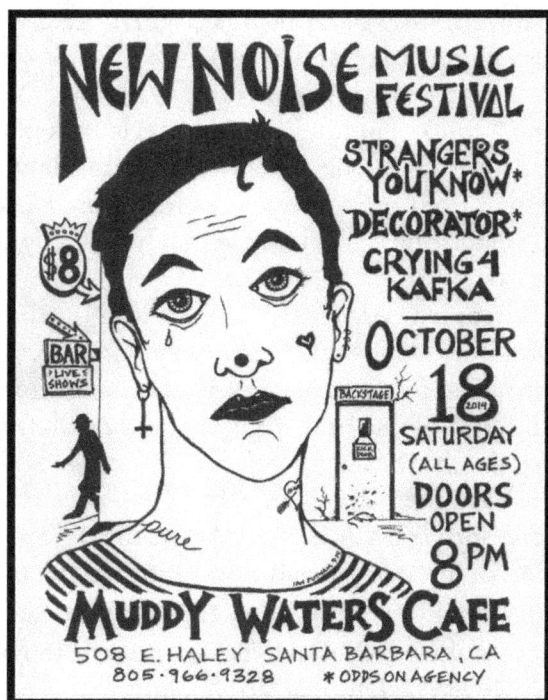

Humbled by the King of Porn

by
Friedrich Nietzsche

One night, December 21st as I recall, having just finished a piece of streusel and a glass of Hefeweissbier, I received a telephone call from a postproduction executive at Nacht-Time Entertainment. Her name was Mila Braun. Hans Nacht, her boss, wanted to meet with me.

Nacht-Time Entertainment was one of the Germany's largest adult video companies. It delivered massive amounts of graphic action with trace elements of plot, generating millions of Euros per month.

I agreed to meet Hans. A private plane took me to Hamburg and brought me back to Leipzig the same evening. My good friend, Goethe, joined us. Goethe had a long a history of defending pornography in novels, essays and poems (e.g. *Die Leiden des jungen Werthers, Sturm und Drang*, and *Faust*).

Hans Nacht was a towering man in his late 30s with spiky blond hair and a thick Hamburgisch accent. He looked like the Soviet gangster from the movie *Brat*. His vice president, Sid Sugar, was a portly man in his mid-50s with a Hugo Boss raincoat nearly two sizes too small. The only evidence that he was cognizant was a whispered growl.

The third member of this troika, sitting in the preposterously long Mercedes Benz limo, was Candy Barr. Ms. Barr, hailing from Cologne, was one of Mr. Nacht's newest stars. Smiling and extending a hand toward me, beauty-pageant style with fingers pointed downward, she drawled, *Pro-fess-orrr Niet-zsche*. Stills from her recent movies were then circulated while I sat transfixed watching mobsters and a porn star talking like effigies in books.

The last of our party, Goethe, was retrieved from Chilehaus. Following cursory introductions, he, too, asked to see the movie stills. (That dieser alte hund). *Wow, look at these*, he remarked, smiling to no one. After we arrived at Parlament Restaurant, Mr. Nacht told his driver to take Ms. Barr to Mönckebergstrasse for a shopping spree. Goethe then launched into an extended monologue about his definition of obscenity (*lacks serious literary, artistic, political, or scientific value*) that became a springboard for his musings about Faust and the witch's kitchen. It didn't help matters that I brought up *Baubo* and *Die fröhliche Wissenschaft*, at which point the entire conversation degenerated into a shouting match.

What's the value of porn? Goethe asked rhetorically. *People like it. It makes them happy,* he loudly said. Then, lamenting the continued prosecution of X-rated films, he mused, *I'm now thinkin' that Hans Nacht should edit his whole damn catalog to reduce his vulnerability to an obscenity conviction.*

This, I learned, was where I came in. Geothe wanted my perspective (as the learned professor, so to speak) so that I could opine about which characteristics should be deleted from Nacht-Time Entertainment videos to offset their purported value. Serving as an expert witness in ensuing Bundesregierung obscenity litigation was part of the arrangement, too.

The real question, then, was whether eliminating objectionable characteristics of pornography would diminish governmental sanctions. Dial-a-porn certainly had managed to gain BNA approval (as I learned in a previous case I had worked on for Deutsche Telekom), but that was largely framed as a freedom of speech issue within the context of a public utility. Devoid of that infrastructure, the question remained whether cultivating an incipient social conscience for pornography, an awareness of the untenable metaphysical or empirical claims about human agency for example, would protect it from obscenity indictments.

Standing on the curb after dinner, Mr. Nacht asked his driver, *Where's Candy?*

I brought her to your schloss, boss, the driver replied.

Taking a deep breath, diamond shimmering in his front tooth, Mr. Nacht screamed, *Scheiße!,* repeating it two more times. *Fuck! FUCK!*

Now facing Goethe and me, Mr. Nacht moaned with regret, *I was going to have her BLOW you guys.*

Blutige Hölle! She'd lovvvvve it, mumbled Sid Sugar.

Damn, Goethe griped instantly, *I would have LOVED it, too!!*

No thanks, is all I said. *I'm meeting Elizabeth for tea.*

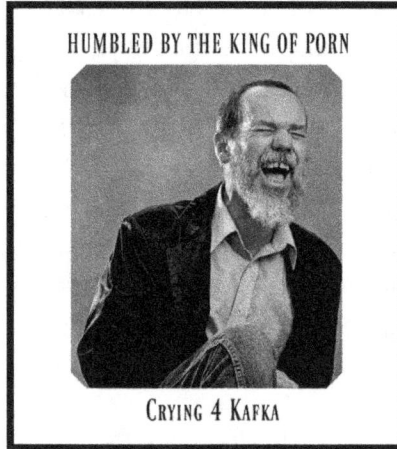

HUMBLED BY THE KING OF PORN

CRYING 4 KAFKA

CASTING PEARLS
BEFORE THE SWINE
CONTEMPT SO VERY CRYSTALLINE
WE WERE WHORES, OR SO HE SAID
AS HE CLIMBED INTO BED

ACTION, CAMERA, SO VERY QUICK
NO REAL SCRUPLES
WITH THESE TRICKS
LEFT TO WEAR THAT CROWN
OF THORNS
HUMBLED BY THE KING OF PORN

Onan's Lament

by
Anne Sexton

Tyranny of the majority is always the death
of Democracy James Madison said.
And said again.
The multitudes dominate
Emma Goldman replied.
Intensified.
Especially to those at night alone,
Married to their beds.

Finger to finger Mary X declaimed
Not far enough she clarified.
Ringing a bell
And raising her voice
An enigma glorified.
At night alone she married her bed.

I break out of my body this way,
Nancy Spero replied.
A dream market
Spread out and crucified.
A little plum is what she meant.
Lingering alone in a conjugal bed.

My black-eyed rival came and went.
Gimme pigfoot and a bottle of beer.
Ivory fingertips,
And amplified lips,
Soon she disappeared.
At night alone she married her bed.

T'aint nobody's business but my own, she said.
T'aint nobody's business but my own.

NIGHTS OF SUFFERING
REMEMBERED WITH LOVE
I KNOW THEY'RE STAGGERING
STAGGERING ABOVE
WORTHLESS TROPHIES
LET ME EXPLAIN
HALF NUDE QUEENS
ALL THE SEX AND GAMES

Bryan Kovarick: I've certainly had more falls and brawls than I wish to recall, but I can still lose myself in the improvisations of a sovereign percussive deity that reigns defiant and sublime.

Evil Knievel: Motorcycling has its own widening ruptures and shatterings of every musical guarantee, *eeeee*-specially them *Snake Canyon Blues*, with my ass suckin' sand on TV.

LIKE FINDING LOVE
IN A VENDING MACHINE

OR PULP FICTION
ON THE SILVER SCREEN

LIKE FINDING LOVE
IN A VENDING MACHINE

AND BEARING WITNESS TO
BROKEN DREAMS

Letter to Franz Kafka

by
Jack Spicer

Dear Franz,

Somehow your letter was no surprise (and I think you knew that it was no surprise or you would have tried to break the news more gently). I think we understood what the other was going to say long before it was said, the overweening scramble for a proof of love and, I think, a protection against the halo of renown. Though I've been expecting this letter for five weeks—I still don't know how to answer it.

San Francisco is a dreadful, wonderful place. It's full of hideous people and beautiful poetry, a stairway of fog into heaven, marvelously multiform and dense, but unfortunately depressing too. It would be wrong of me to drag a person I love into such a place against his will. Unless you walk into it freely, and with open despairing eyes, perhaps you won't even see the fog but will fix your gaze instead upon the historical textures and the celebrated layers of weather.

And yet I can't leave San Francisco myself to come to you—San Francisco is inside of me, in a sense it is me, and was the price I paid, and the oath I signed to write songs.

I think that someday you'll enter San Francisco—not for me (I'm not worth the price, no human being is), but for poetry—to see the fog without noticing how ransacked and pauperized it can be, and then hopefully blast yourself through the rocks of hell. I'll be there waiting for you, my arms open to receive you.

Let's have these letters continue for days, years, or however long it is before I see you again. We can still love each other, consummately sly at least, but beautifully translated from alien worlds – Prague and San Francisco - despite being thousands of miles apart.

Love, Jack

[*c.1951-2*]

I AM ME, AS YOU ARE ME
AS WE ARE FREE, AND WE ARE ALL
TRANSGRESSORS
SEE HOW THEY RUN, LIKE VAMPIRES
FROM THE SUN
SEE HOW THEY DIE
I'M CRYING....4 KAFKA

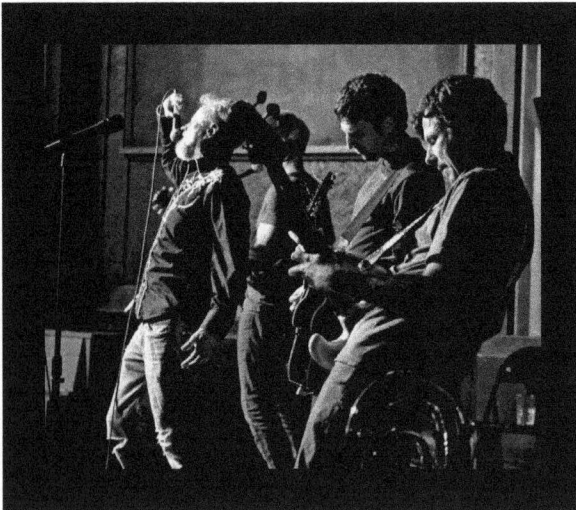

THE SAINT OF FUCKED UP KARMA

Erika Blair
The Americana Desolation Music Academy
Joshua Tree, California

The title is not gratuitous. The story was true and over-whelmingly fucked up. It involved a police officer caught in the act of raping a 13-year-old boy. It got worse from there. Though the details are true, the names and places are not, transforming the despicable into something more accessible - albeit in anguished sort of way - as if parable and annihilation were joined at the hip. The curses of Nepenthe, the fates of Salome, the cries from Kafka are all peculiar unto themselves, desperate voices of humanity that hail the regrettable continuity of tragedy while *preachin' the truth at the crossroads of our sins.*

The first scene is below.

Scene 1

Dr. Frank Matthews (Begins his monologue about Porter Jones):

People tell me that I'm a saint for getting involved in these cases. I've never seen it that way. I'm just better at staying detached. It's a blessing—and a curse. (Pauses)

His name was Porter Jones. He was 13 years old. His mother, Dolly, was a prostitute; his father, Jake, was a bank robber who had OD'd on heroin soon after he got out of jail.

Dolly was done. Done with dope. Done with bank robbers. Done with Johns. She had moved to a tiny town near Sedona, Arizona, to get away from it all. She thought she had it made when a friendly cop, Tim Tully, took an interest in her son.

(Dr. Matthews acts this part out:)
How old are you?
13
That's close enough. Come on! Want to join the Police Ex-plorers? Ya get a uniform, a badge. Teach you to shoot a gun. You ever shot a gun? Fun as hell!
No! But yeah! said Porter.

Three months go by. Porter is in the Explorers, and Tim Tully lavishes Dolly with gifts, a laptop, all kinds of stuff.

Then one night Tully asks Dolly:

(Dr. Matthews acts this part out:)
Hey, I'm having a barbecue. Next Friday night. We got tri-tip. We're gonna ride ATVs. My old girlfriend'll be there. Can Porter come? It'll be great! He can spend the night.

Dolly thinks, Sure, that's fine; he's a cop.

Tim Tully has the barbecue, they eat tri-tip, they ride the ATVs, but at ten thirty, Tully's old girlfriend leaves.

Sixteen miles later her car breaks down. Tully's house is closer than Flagstaff, so she has it towed back to his home.

Something's not quite right. Sheets are covering the windows. She uses her key to open the front door and walks inside.

Right there on the couch Tim Tully is raping Porter Jones.

Tully jumps up. Grabs his gun. Puts it to her head.

She WAILS. Just WAILS.

He puts the gun to his own head. She WAILS even louder.

Tully throws down the gun, calls his department chief, and confesses.

There are three distinct arcs to this musical. The story of Porter, Dolly, and Tim Tully comprise the first arc. The second arc explores the impact of working on cases that involve deplorable crimes. Is Dr. Matthews, for example, still capable of intimacy in his personal life? Keely, his girlfriend, is the device for exploring this question.

The third arc, no less important than the first, explains

how Dr. Matthews became involved in this work—not merely the referrals, but how he learned to thrive therein despite the obstructing indictments, the idolatrous venerations, and the bigotry and contempt. The second and third arcs are evident in Scenes 2 and 3 below.

Scene 2

Keely: Do you ever get burned out?
Dr. Matthews: What do ya mean?
Keely: Your crazy childhood. The world of trauma?
Dr. Matthews: I'd beware of pity.
Keely: Pity? It's not pity. It's concern. Your life is enshrined in grief. (Pauses) I know you're fighting for something. Who could miss that? But it all gets mixed up in a twisted kind of way.
Dr. Matthews: I give to these people.
Keely: Your cases. But not to me. Or us.
Dr. Matthews: I see it differently. You thrive on hope. I don't. I don't believe in soul mates. Marriages made in heaven. I can't imagine how any of those things could yield happiness. I want none of it.
Keely: What's wrong with soul mates?
Dr. Matthews: Nothing. Nothing. I just don't believe in them. I look around. Everyone is falling in or out of love. I'm done with it.
Keely: That's depressing.
Dr. Matthews: Things I do, or try to do, are done because I think they're right. It's gotta feel right. Marriage is a crapshoot. I don't like to gamble.
Keely: Is it right between us?
Dr. Matthews: Definitely! Definitely!
Keely: Then why'd you disappear? For three weeks? No calls. Nothing!
Dr. Matthews: I had no choice. I keep telling you that. I had no choice. This case . . .
Keely: You're always on cases.
Dr. Matthews: Not like this one. Cop raping a kid. Can you

105

imagine? Mother is a prostitute. He needed help.

Keely: We need help.

Dr. Matthews: That cop knew exactly what he was doing. This family had billboards on their backs: **WOUNDED BIRDS.**

Keely: I don't doubt any of that. But it's beside the point. We're a sinking ship. We deserve better.

Dr. Matthews: We're not sinking. Just because I don't feel the way you do doesn't mean that I care any less. (Pauses) You're an artist. You're always seeing things differently. (Pauses) I never know what to do. Keep talking or go for a walk. (Pauses) It's not for the lack of trying. I just never know what to do. I can't figure it out.

Scene 3

Dr. Frank Matthews (Begins a monologue about his childhood):

I was in a terrible accident. I was eight years old. (Lifts his shirt to show the scar.) Fifty stitches. The scar runs from below my belly button to my rib cage, and then it turns right, toward my back. It looks like a jagged lowercase r. Imagine it on an 8-year-old. And angry red.

I was standing on a five-foot ledge. I slipped and fell to the concrete below and was knocked unconscious. Another kid fell, too. His knees landed in my stomach. I was dead, or so he thought. He ran away.

When I woke up, I crawled home on both arms, dragging my body behind me, blood dripping from my mouth.

It freaked the hell out of my mother. An ambulance was called, and it took me to Saint Agatha's Hospital. The Emergency Room doctor looked like Sherlock Holmes—not the new actor, but the old one, Basil Rathbone. He was holding an enormous needle.

Frank, he whispered, *you won't feel a thing.*

I didn't.

But I did remember what my father said to me in the ambulance.

You know what the FUCK this is going to cost me?!

Run, Frank, run is all I could think.

Though perhaps it's hard to imagine how this case could have gotten worse, the final scene is also included herein. Looking for a loophole in a feudal morality, eschewing the constraints of social cohesion, hounded and castigated for a love affair with drugs and violence, and provoked by a steady stream of persecution and revilement, how could this drama end otherwise? The music, no less than the story itself, is a fitting destination for an Americana Desolation punk rock band.

Scene 14

Dr. Matthews (Completes his monologue about Porter Jones):
Four years after Porter got out of federal prison, I got a call from a public defender in Albuquerque, New Mexico. Her name was Alba Woods. She asked me if I knew Porter.
(**Dr. Matthews** acts out the phone call:)
    Dr. Matthews: Yeah. I know him.
    Alba Woods: He says he was sexually molested by a police officer. Is that true?
    Dr. Matthews: Yeah. I got all the paperwork.
    Alba Woods: Would you be willing to tell that to a jury?
    Dr. Matthews: Why a jury?
    Alba Woods: Porter Jones has been arrested for a terrible, terrible crime. He kidnapped and raped a 10 year-old girl. Will you please, PLEASE, tell the jury that he did it because of that cop?!?
    Dr. Matthews (loudly): NO! I'm not going to do that! No way. That card has been played! It's done!! I can't tell you how many times we bailed him out of Juvi. And the misery and heartache of watching him blow through the money— only to end up in prison for armed robbery.
    This guy thinks he's immune from punishment. He's on his own. I'm done. No agonized tributes to redemption. This is about accountability! Porter is on the hook for this one!
    Dr. Matthews (Looking directly at the audience):
Porter Jones was convicted and given a 100-year sentence without parole.

Witnesses saw him kidnap the little girl off the street. The police immediately gave chase. Up and down a windy mountain road. Porter is driving so fast that he goes off a cliff and rolls down into a ditch. Police don't realize it at first; they keep on driving.

Nobody is hurt. Porter climbs out of the car. It's real quiet. He thinks he's home free. He then rapes the little girl in the upended car. Can you believe that?

A year's worth of documentary filmmaking by Verité TV followed thereafter. An emancipation cradled in enlightenment that focused upon the problems of allegiance; a promulgation of the grand principle that choice and the liberty of conscience are the foundations of an all-inclusive moral compass, coupled of course with a civilizing and spacious need to do what's right regardless of the consequences.

Like most documentaries, however, it was never finished.

HERE'S A TRUTH I KNOW
GOLDEN CALF EVER AGLOW

EVEN WORSE, I ABHOR
DUELING GODS WANTING MORE

WAR, STARVATION, MISERY VAST
TIME TO MAKE, THING OF THE PAST

DREAM THE DREAM
WE CAN'T IGNORE
BANGING HARD ON EVERY DOOR

CANONIZED, HYPNOTIZED
HUMAN RIGHTS CRUCIFIED

CANONIZED, HYPNOTIZED
HUMAN RIGHTS CRUCIFIED

CANONIZED, HYPNOTIZED, HUMAN
RIGHTS CRUCIFIED

CANONIZED, HYPNOTIZED, HUMAN
RIGHTS CRUCIFIED

crying 4 kafka
(acoustic)

Sunday
12/3/17

4pm.
Free

A. G. Geiger Fine Art Books
502 Chung King Ct. LA, CA. 90012
Chinatown

Coda

Erika Blair
The Americana Desolation Music Academy
Joshua Tree, California

When Crying 4 Kafka – its essence, its oeuvre, its metaphysic – entered musical discourse in so urgent a manner it renewed, if not inflamed, rock and roll. Relying upon a disquisition of punk, conceptual sweep, and metrical flair it emerged as a musical anomaly that profoundly engaged an idiom that became the expositor of Americana desolation punk rock. It's impossible to conceive of any other musical forum drawn to such an illuminating reconsideration of raw sonic power and lyrical sledgehammers that relegated conventional song to perplexing and superannuated trivia. At some point contemporary music will be indebted to the idioms and cadences of Crying 4 Kafka - the indelible voice and irretrievable sounds that stand as venerable legacies, exalting, dazzling, and strange. Songs that are testimonies to skepticism, choice and dissent, with occasional forays into ruthless condemnations and sacral dissections, the unacknowledged pits of humanity so to speak, all of which is combined into an enduring template of renegade liturgy.

TESTIMONY IS NEVER SYNONYMOUS WITH EXPERIENCE.

**I WILL FIND THE ANSWER
I WILL FIND THE WAY
I STAND AS A WITNESS
NEVER TO BETRAY**

**TEMPTATION ALL AROUND US
PATH AIN'T ALWAYS CLEAR
I STAND AS A WITNESS
A CHALLENGE TO THE FEAR**

DRAMATIS PERSONAE

Paul R. Abramson
(vocals and lyrics)

Ian Putnam *(guitar)*	Marc Bobro *(bass, tuba)*	Bryan Kovarick *(drums)*

Ian Putnam *(guitar)*	Marc Bobro *(bass, tuba)*	Cedric Bobro *(drums)*

Ian Putnam *(lead guitar)*	Mattia Bacca *(rhythm guitar)*	Marc Bobro *(bass, tuba)*	Dave Rios *(drums)*

Ian Putnam *(lead guitar)*	Mattia Bacca *(rhythm guitar)*	Marc Bobro *(bass, tuba)*	Brandon Thibeault *(drums)*

Jesse Burrill *(guitar)*	Marc Bobro *(bass)*	Brandon Thibeault *(drums)*

Rick Ambrose *(guitar)*	Marc Bobro *(bass)*	Brandon Thibeault *(drums)*

Steve Stewart *(guitar)*	Marc Bobro *(bass)*	Brandon Thibeault *(drums)*

Steve Stewart *(lead guitar)*	Tim Cooley *(rhythm guitar)*	Marc Bobro *(bass)*	Brandon Thibeault *(drums)*

Steve Stewart *(guitar)*	Marc Bobro *(bass)*	Brandon Thibeault *(drums)*

Steve Stewart *(guitar)*	Chas Thompson *(bass)*	Brandon Thibeault *(drums)*

Steve Stewart *(guitar)*	Joe Dean *(bass)*	Brandon Thibeault *(drums)*

Steve Stewart *(guitar)*	Joe Dean *(bass)*	Barry Birmingham *(drums)*

GUESTS:

Tania Love Abramson (*background vocals*)
CeLaLa (*background vocals*)
Robin Finck (*guitar*)
Cate Imperio (*impresario*)
The Qwyire (Terri Cruz & Molly Poiset) – (*background vocals*)
Dave Raven (*drums*)

ROADIES:

Keith V. Abramson
Eric Ray Andrade Santiago

MASTERING:

Paul du Gre
Ian Putnam

PRODUCERS:

Paul Abramson and Ian Putnam
Paul Abramson and Steve Stewart
Paul du Gre

RECORDING:

Paul Abramson
Paul du Gre
Ian Putnam
Steve Stewart

RECORDING STUDIOS:

Paul & Mike's Recording Studio, Burbank, California
      (Paul du Gre, Proprietor)
Vending Machine Sound, Santa Barbara, California
      (Ian Putnam, Proprietor)

RECORD LABELS:

Hellflowers in LA Records
Waiting for Godzilla Records

MUSIC PUBLISHING COMPANY:

She Stabbed Moses Music

GOSPEL CHOIR (for The Sacred and the Profane Show):

Mama Pat's Inner Light Gospel Choir, Santa Barbara, California

ACTORS (for The Saint of Fucked-Up Karma):

Paul Abramson, Emma Bobro, Terri Cruz, Melanie Eckford-Prossor,
Ian Putnam, Sean Vancleve, Linda Williamson.

OF COUNSEL:

Terry Gross, J.D. of the law firm Gross & Belsky

CRYING 4 KAFKA: YOUTUBE

CRYING 4 KAFKA: FACEBOOK

CRYING 4 KAFKA: ITUNES

CRYING 4 KAFKA: SINGLES (on iTunes)

Contemplating Whores Again
Crying for Kafka (2017)
Fuck Mom/Fuck Dad (2017)
Give Sodomy a Chance (2018)
Holy Roller
Human Rights Crucified
I Can Speak for Myself
I Want Magnificence (2017)
Like Finding Love in a Vending Machine
Oh God/No God
Run Frank Run
The Saint of Fucked-Up Karma
Win Big (with Tuba)

CRYING 4 KAFKA: CDs:

Humbled by the King of Porn (2014, Hellflowers in LA Records)
(*Prologue, We'd Do the Time, Unchain Verite', Humbled by the King of Porn, Sex and Games, I Was Gonna Have Her Blow You Guys, Hide Your Gun, Mistaken Queen, She Stabbed Moses, Epilogue.*)

The Frank Recordings (2012, Hellflowers in LA Records) (*Run Frank Run, Win Big & Lose It All, Holy Roller, Hey, I'm Not Sorry, Punching at Your Heart, Commuters Liquor Store.*)

Live @ Stockmal (2012, Hellflowers in LA Records) (*I Can Speak for Myself, American President Loves His War, Crying for Kafka, I Want Magnificence, Fuck Mom/Fuck Dad, Run Frank Run, Holy Roller, Nothing Looked True, So, So So, LA, When Hate Becomes Commonplace, I'm Going to Live the Life, Give Sodomy A Chance, A Madman Sings, Drugs & Drama, and Demons Come Dance.*)

Rage & Misery (2011, Waiting for Godzilla Records) (*Rage & Misery, Near Enough to Spark, Drugs and Drama, Where Left is Always Right, Contemplating Whores, Matter of Fact (remix), Madison.*)

God is Dead and We Survive: (2010, Waiting for Godzilla Records) (*Crying for Kafka, A Madman Sings, When Hate Becomes Commonplace, Lost Moments, I'm Going to Live the Life, Words We Forever Seek, Behind the Clouds, Matter of Fact, Nothing Looked True, Give Sodomy A Chance, George Carlin's Lament, Too Much.*)

Ain't Always Paradise: (2009, Waiting for Godzilla Records) (*Ain't Always Paradise, American President Loved His War, Fuck Mom/Fuck Dad, Human Rights Brutalized, Demons Come Dance, Circus Mind, I Want Magnificence, Pride to Swallow, Watchmaker's Dial.*)

SELECTED VENUES:

A.G. Geiger Art Bookstore (*Chinatown, LA, CA*), **Beauty Bar** (*Las Vegas, NV*), **BG Gallery** (*LA, CA*), **BoHenry's** (*Santa Barbara, CA*), **Club Fais Do Do** (*LA, CA*), **Cold Spring Tavern** (*Santa Barbara, CA*), **Chung King Court** (*Chinatown, LA, CA*), **Double Down** (*Las Vegas, NV*), **Dr. Susan Block's Sex Club** (*LA, CA*), **Glassbox Gallery** (*Department of Art, UCSB, Santa Barbara, CA*) **Green Art People** (*Ventura, CA*), **Halloween House Party** (*LA, CA*), **House of Blues on Sunset Strip** (*LA, CA*), **Jensen's Main Stage** (*Santa Barbara, CA*) **King King** (*LA, CA*), **Malibu Plains** (*Malibu, CA*), **Muddy Waters** (*Santa Barbara, CA*), **On the Rox** (*LA, CA)*, **Reds** (*Santa Barbara, CA*), **Red Cove** (*Ventura, CA*), **Soho** (*Santa Barbara, CA*), **Sans Souci** (*Ventura, CA*), **The Frog and the Peach** (*San Luis Obispo, CA*), **The Garage** (*Ventura, CA*), **The Joshua Tree Saloon** (*Joshua Tree, CA*), **The Mint** (*LA, CA*), **The Railway Club** (*Vancouver, BC*), **The Rainbow Room on Sunset Strip** (*LA, CA*), **The Roxy on Sunset Strip** (*LA, CA*), **The Viper Room on Sunset Strip** (*LA, CA*), **The Mark Orlando Woodworks Warehouse** (*Santa Barbara, CA*), **The Water Tower** (*Santa Barbara, CA*), **UCLA Radio** (*LA, CA*), **UCSB Radio** (*Santa Barbara, CA*), **Velvet Jones** (*Santa Barbara, CA*), **Whiskey Richards** (*Santa Barbara, CA*).

CREDITS

Cover   Painting by Paul R. Abramson, 2010.

pg. 7   Photograph by Tania Love Abramson, 2018.

pg. 10   Sketches (*guitar, mic*) by Paul R. Abramson, 2018.

pg. 11   Sketches (*euphonium, drums*) by Paul R. Abramson, 2018.

pg. 13   Photograph by Ann Purdy, (from the film *Regret is My Demon*), 2008.

pg. 16   Posters by Wallace Piatt, 2010.

pg. 19   Photograph by Tania Love Abramson, 2016.

pg. 22   Flyer by Paul R. Abramson, 2018.

pg. 26   Photograph by Sienna Bland-Abramson, 2013.

Erika Blair

www.ingramcontent.com/pod-product-compliance
Lightning Source LLC
Chambersburg PA
CBHW031536040426
42445CB00010B/563